150

INDIAN
recipes

INSPIRED IDEAS FOR
EVERYDAY COOKING

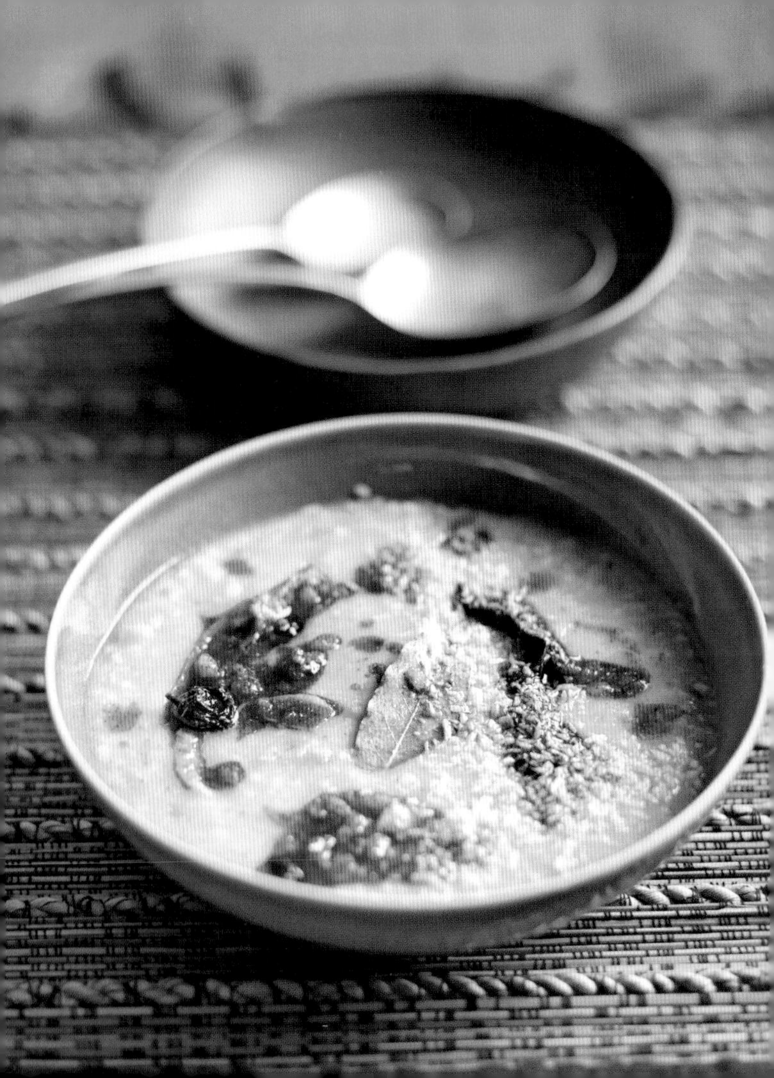

CONTENTS

INTRODUCTION

Indian food is one of our most popular cuisines and increasingly people enjoy creating a wide variety of authentic Indian dishes at home. It's no surprise then that curry is one of our nation's favourite foods.

Indian cookery varies across the vast expanse of the country, with each region having its own specialities. A wide range of curries can be found throughout India and they too differ from region to region – some are creamy and mild, such as Korma, others like Madras tend to be medium-hot, while curries such as Vindaloo are really hot and spicy.

We include a delicious collection of really tempting recipes that will set your senses ablaze and tantalize your taste buds. Many dishes are quick and easy to make, so can be on the table faster than your average takeaway,

and they promise to deliver minimum preparation and maximum flavour!

Super starters and accompaniments include a sizzling selection of chutneys, raitas, pakoras and bhajis, plus other delights such as Masala Prawn Cakes (see page 42) and Bombay Potatoes (see page 54).

Mighty main courses include a wide variety of vegetable, pulse, meat, fish and seafood dishes, such as everyday classics like Sag Aloo (see page 80), Chicken Tikka Masala (see page 110) and Beef Madras (see page 142). If you are keen on entertaining, recipes such as Pistachio Chicken Korma (see page 108), Marinated Lamb Brochettes (see page 129) and Lobster Cooked Beach-style (see page 204) are sure to impress your guests.

To complete our collection, we include a tempting choice of rice, breads and sweet dishes, featuring popular recipes such as Pilau Rice (see page 210), Chapatis (see page 226) and Naan Bread (see page 228), as well as some satisfying treats for those with a sweet tooth, including Creamy Almond, Pistachio and Rice Pudding (see page 242) and Sweet Lassi (see page 252).

Indian food is packed full of flavour and colour, the emphasis tending to be on main course dishes, with several dishes selected to complement each other and be served together. Indian dishes, including many curries, are usually served with a range of appetizing accompaniments, including naan bread, chapatis, parathas, pooris, simple boiled or flavoured rice such as pilau or biryani, chutneys, relishes, pickles and raitas. Soup may also be served and sweet dishes can be enjoyed for special occasions or for a mid-morning or afternoon treat. Refreshing drinks such as lassis are also popular.

Flavours in Indian cookery vary from lightly spiced dhals and rice dishes to some much more robustly flavoured dishes, including the many different curries. Spices are essential in many Indian recipes to create the wonderfully balanced and fragrant dishes. Popular spices used are wide-ranging and include cardamom, chillies, cinnamon, cloves, coriander, cumin, curry leaves, fennel and fenugreek seeds, ginger, mustard seeds, saffron, tamarind, turmeric, and many more.

To enjoy the authentic flavours of home-cooked Indian food, buy good quality whole spices and grind them yourself using a clean electric coffee grinder (kept specifically for spices), a spice grinder or pestle and mortar. Buy whole spices in relatively small quantities so they don't go stale, and grind them fresh each time to enjoy their finest flavour. If you do use ready-ground spices, be sure to keep them in airtight containers or jars in a cool, dark, dry place, and replace them every 6 months or so, as they deteriorate quite quickly and lose their fresh flavour.

Dry-frying whole spices in a heavy-based frying pan for a few minutes or until they release their delicious fragrances before grinding them, will also bring out their aromatic flavour and vastly improve the taste of your dishes.

By combining a selection of fresh ingredients and key spices, you can create many of the much-loved spicy and fragrant Indian dishes in your very own kitchen.

INTRODUCTION

STARTERS & SIDES

CUCUMBER RAITA

Serves: 4

Prep: 15 mins,
plus cooling

Cook: 2–3 mins

Ingredients

1 small cucumber
175 g/6 oz natural yogurt
¼ tsp granulated sugar
¼ tsp salt
1 tsp cumin seeds
10–12 black peppercorns
¼ tsp paprika

Method

1 Peel the cucumber and scoop out the seeds. Cut the flesh into bite-sized pieces and set aside.

2 Put the yogurt into a bowl and beat with a fork until smooth. Add the sugar and salt, and mix well.

3 Heat a small, heavy-based saucepan over a medium–high heat. When the pan is hot, turn off the heat and add the cumin seeds and peppercorns. Stir constantly for 40–50 seconds, until they release their aroma.

4 Remove from the pan and leave to cool for 5 minutes, then crush in a spice grinder or mortar.

5 Reserve ¼ teaspoon of this mixture and stir the remainder into the yogurt. Add the cucumber and stir to mix. Transfer the raita to a small serving bowl and sprinkle with the reserved toasted spices and the paprika.

★ **Variation**

For a delicious cooling effect, add some finely chopped fresh mint with the cucumber.

MANGO & PINEAPPLE RAITA

Serves: 4

Prep: 15 mins,
plus optional chilling

Cook: 2 mins

Ingredients

250 g/9 oz natural yogurt

1 onion, finely sliced

1 tomato, finely chopped

1 fresh green chilli, finely chopped

100 g/3½ oz pineapple flesh, finely diced

100 g/3½ oz ripe mango flesh, finely diced

¼ tsp salt

2 tbsp vegetable or groundnut oil

1 tsp black mustard seeds

4 fresh curry leaves

Method

1 Place the yogurt in a bowl and whisk until smooth.

2 Add the onion, tomato, chilli, pineapple, mango and salt to the yogurt and stir to mix well.

3 Heat the oil in a small frying pan, then add the mustard seeds and curry leaves. Cook, stirring constantly for a few seconds, or until the mustard seeds start to pop.

4 Remove the pan from the heat and pour the contents over the yogurt mixture. Stir gently to combine and serve immediately, or chill until required.

CRISPY OKRA RAITA

Serves: 4   **Prep: 10-15 mins**   **Cook: 6-8 mins**

Ingredients

6 tbsp vegetable or groundnut oil

200 g/7 oz okra, trimmed and cut into 1-cm/½-inch slices

400 g/14 oz natural yogurt

1 tsp salt

1 tsp sugar

1 tsp cayenne pepper

¼ tsp ground turmeric

1 tsp black mustard seeds

2 tbsp finely chopped fresh coriander

Method

1 Heat 5 tablespoons of the oil in a large frying pan over a medium heat. When the oil is very hot, add the okra, toss and cook, stirring occasionally, for 3–4 minutes – the okra will slowly turn crispy and brown. Once the okra is well browned, transfer to kitchen paper to drain and set aside until ready to serve.

2 Whisk the yogurt with the salt and sugar in a medium-sized serving bowl. Sprinkle the cayenne pepper and turmeric over the yogurt mixture, but do not mix it in.

3 Heat the remaining oil in a small frying pan over a high heat. When the oil begins to smoke, add the mustard seeds. When the mustard seeds stop popping, pour the hot oil directly on top of the cayenne pepper and turmeric. (This will cook the spices without burning them.)

4 Just before serving, place the crispy okra on top and scatter over the chopped coriander.

MANGO CHUTNEY

Makes: 250 g/9 oz

Prep: 15 mins,
plus cooling & chilling

Cook: 15–20 mins

Ingredients

400 g/14 oz ripe mango
flesh, finely diced

2 tbsp lime juice

1 tbsp vegetable or
groundnut oil

2 shallots, finely chopped

1 garlic clove,
finely chopped

2 fresh green chillies,
deseeded and finely sliced

1 tsp black mustard seeds

1 tsp coriander seeds

5 tbsp grated jaggery
or soft light brown sugar

5 tbsp white wine vinegar

1 tsp salt

pinch of ground ginger

Method

1 Put the mango in a mixing bowl with the lime
juice and set aside.

2 Heat the oil in a large frying pan over a
medium–high heat. Add the shallots and cook
for 3 minutes. Add the garlic and chillies and stir
for a further 2 minutes, or until the shallots are
softened, but not browned. Add the mustard
and coriander seeds, and stir to combine.

3 Add the mango to the pan with the jaggery,
vinegar, salt and ground ginger, and mix well.
Reduce the heat to its lowest setting and simmer
for 10 minutes, until the liquid thickens and the
mango becomes sticky.

4 Remove from the heat and leave to cool
completely. Once cool, transfer to an
airtight container, cover and chill for 3 days
before serving.

TAMARIND CHUTNEY

Makes: 250 g/9 oz

Prep: 15 mins, plus cooling & chilling

Cook: 40 mins

Ingredients

100 g/3½ oz tamarind pulp, chopped

450 ml/16 fl oz water

½ fresh bird's eye chilli, or to taste, deseeded and chopped

55 g/2 oz soft light brown sugar, or to taste

½ tsp salt

Method

1 Put the tamarind and water in a heavy-based saucepan over a high heat, and bring to the boil. Reduce the heat to its lowest setting and simmer for 25 minutes, stirring occasionally to break up the tamarind pulp, or until tender.

2 Tip the tamarind pulp into a sieve and quickly place the sieve back on top of the empty saucepan. Use a wooden spoon to push the pulp through the sieve into the pan.

3 Add the chilli, sugar and salt to the sieved tamarind mixture and continue to simmer for a further 10 minutes, or until the chutney thickens. Leave to cool slightly, then stir in extra sugar or salt, to taste.

4 Leave to cool completely, then transfer to an airtight container and chill for up to 3 days before serving as a dipping sauce or accompaniment.

CORIANDER CHUTNEY

Serves: 4

Prep: 20 mins,
plus optional chilling

Cook: No cooking

Ingredients

1½ tbsp lemon juice

1½ tbsp cold water

85 g/3 oz fresh coriander leaves and stems, roughly chopped

2 tbsp chopped fresh coconut

1 small shallot, very finely chopped

5-mm/¼-inch piece fresh ginger, chopped

1 fresh green chilli, deseeded and chopped

½ tsp sugar, or to taste

½ tsp salt, or to taste

pinch of pepper, or to taste

Method

1 Put the lemon juice and water in a food processor. Add half the coriander and process until it is blended and a slushy paste forms. Gradually add the remaining coriander and process until it is all blended, scraping down the sides of the processor, if necessary. If you don't have a processor suitable for this small quantity, use a pestle and mortar, adding the coriander in small amounts.

2 Add the remaining ingredients and continue processing until they are all finely chopped and blended. Taste and adjust the seasoning, adding extra sugar and salt if needed. Transfer to a serving bowl and serve immediately, or cover and chill until required.

STARTERS & SIDES

LIME PICKLE

Makes: 225 g/8 oz

Prep: 20 mins,
plus standing, cooling
& storing

Cook: 2–3 mins

Ingredients

12 limes, halved and deseeded

115 g/4 oz salt

70 g/2½ oz chilli powder

25 g/1 oz mustard powder

25 g/1 oz ground fenugreek

1 tbsp ground turmeric

300 ml/10 fl oz mustard oil

15 g/½ oz yellow mustard seeds, crushed

½ tsp asafoetida

Method

1 Cut each lime half into four pieces and pack them into a large, sterilized jar, sprinkling over the salt as you go. Cover and leave to stand in a warm place for 10–14 days, or until the limes have turned brown and softened.

2 Mix together the chilli and mustard powders, fenugreek and turmeric in a small bowl and add to the jar of limes. Stir to mix, then re-cover and leave to stand for a further 2 days.

3 Transfer the lime mixture to a heatproof bowl. Heat the mustard oil in a heavy-based frying pan.

4 Add the mustard seeds and asafoetida to the pan and cook, stirring constantly, until the oil is very hot and just beginning to smoke. Pour the oil and spices over the limes and mix well. Cover and leave to cool. When cool, pack back into a sterilized jar, seal and store in a sunny place for 1 week before serving.

GREEN CHILLI PICKLE

Serves: 4–6

Prep: 25 mins,
plus storing

Cook: 2–3 mins

Ingredients

20 fresh green chillies

3 tbsp ground coriander

1–1½ tbsp fennel seeds

1 tsp fenugreek seeds

1 tsp black mustard seeds

pinch of asafoetida

3 tsp salt

1 tsp dried mango powder (amchoor)

½ tsp ground turmeric

4 tbsp mustard oil

2 tbsp white wine vinegar

Method

1 Wash and dry the chillies and cut a slit lengthways in each.

2 Place the ground coriander, fennel seeds, fenugreek seeds and mustard seeds in a spice grinder or mortar and grind coarsely. Transfer to a bowl.

3 Add the asafoetida, salt, dried mango powder and turmeric, and mix well.

4 Heat the oil in a frying pan until hot, then stir in the spice mixture. Cook, stirring constantly, for 1 minute and remove from the heat. Add the vinegar and stir to mix well.

5 Stuff the chillies with the spice mixture and pack into a large, sterilized jar. Seal and store in a warm place (preferably on a sunny kitchen windowsill) for up to 2 days before serving.

STARTERS & SIDES

COCONUT SAMBAL

Serves: 4

Prep: 15–25 mins, plus optional chilling

Cook: No cooking

Ingredients

½ fresh coconut or
125 g/4½ oz desiccated
coconut

2 fresh green chillies,
chopped, and deseeded
if liked

2.5-cm/1-inch piece fresh
ginger, finely chopped

4 tbsp chopped
fresh coriander

2 tbsp lemon juice,
or to taste

2 shallots, very finely
chopped

Method

1 If you are using a whole, fresh coconut, use a hammer and nail to punch a hole in the 'eye' of the coconut, then pour out the water from inside and reserve. Use the hammer to break the coconut in half, then peel and chop one half.

2 Put the chopped coconut and the chillies in a food processor and process for about 30 seconds, until finely chopped. Add the ginger, coriander and lemon juice, and process again.

3 If the mixture seems too dry, stir in about 1 tablespoon of the reserved coconut water or water. Stir in the shallots and serve immediately, or cover and chill in the refrigerator until required.

SPICED YOGURT SOUP

Serves: 4   **Prep: 20 mins**   **Cook: 15–20 mins**

Ingredients

1 litre/1¾ pints cold water

500 g/1 lb 2 oz natural yogurt

3 tbsp gram flour

4 fresh green chillies, slit lengthways

1 tbsp freshly grated ginger

1 tbsp palm sugar

1 tsp ground turmeric

1 tbsp vegetable or groundnut oil

1 tbsp ghee

2 dried red chillies, broken into pieces

8 fresh curry leaves

1 tsp cumin seeds

½ tsp black mustard seeds

pinch of asafoetida

4 tbsp chopped fresh coriander

salt

Method

1 Mix together the water, yogurt and gram flour in a large saucepan until smooth. Add the green chillies, ginger, palm sugar, turmeric and salt to taste. Bring the mixture to the boil, then immediately reduce the heat to low and cook, stirring frequently, for 8–10 minutes. Remove from the heat and set aside.

2 Meanwhile, heat the oil and ghee in a small frying pan over a medium heat. Add the dried red chillies, curry leaves, cumin and mustard seeds, and asafoetida, and cook, stirring constantly, for 2–3 minutes, or until the seeds start to pop.

3 Stir the spiced oil into the yogurt mixture in the saucepan. Ladle into warm bowls, scatter over the coriander and serve hot.

SPICED CHICKPEA & SPINACH SOUP

Serves: 4   **Prep: 10 mins**   **Cook: 25–30 mins**

Ingredients

1 tbsp vegetable or groundnut oil

1 onion, finely chopped

2 garlic cloves, crushed

1 tsp cumin seeds

2 tsp medium curry powder

1 tsp hot chilli powder

400 g/14 oz canned cooked chickpeas, drained

400 g/14 oz canned chopped tomatoes

500 ml/18 fl oz vegetable stock

100 g/3½ oz spinach, de-stalked and chopped

salt and pepper, to taste

Mint dressing

100 g/3½ oz natural yogurt

2 tbsp finely chopped fresh mint

Method

1 Heat the oil in a large, heavy-based saucepan over a medium heat. Add the onion and sauté for 4–5 minutes, or until starting to soften.

2 Add the garlic, cumin seeds, curry and chilli powders and cook for 1 minute, stirring constantly.

3 Add the chickpeas, tomatoes and stock, and season to taste with salt and pepper. Bring to the boil, then reduce the heat, cover and simmer for 15 minutes.

4 Meanwhile, to make the mint dressing, mix the yogurt and mint together in a small bowl with salt and pepper, to taste. Cover and chill until ready to serve.

5 Stir the spinach into the soup and cook for a further 1–2 minutes, or until the spinach has wilted. Serve hot with a little of the mint dressing drizzled over.

SAVOURY CHEESE CAKES

Makes: 8

Prep: 20 mins, plus soaking

Cook: 25 mins

Ingredients

2 large slices day-old bread

225 g/8 oz paneer, grated

3 shallots, finely chopped

1 tsp fennel seeds

½ tsp cumin seeds

1 tbsp chopped fresh mint

2 tbsp chopped fresh coriander

1 tsp ginger purée

25 g/1 oz flaked almonds

1 fresh green chilli, chopped

½ tsp garam masala

½ tsp chilli powder

½ tsp salt, or to taste

1 tbsp lemon juice

1 large egg, beaten

vegetable or groundnut oil, for shallow-frying

Method

1 Remove the crusts from the bread and soak in a bowl of water for 1–2 minutes, then squeeze out the water and crumble the slices between your palms into a large bowl. Add all the remaining ingredients, except the oil. Mix well to form a binding consistency.

2 Divide the mixture in half and shape each half into 4 equal-sized flat cakes 5 mm/¼ inch thick.

3 Heat enough oil for shallow-frying in a large frying pan over a medium heat. Add the cakes, working in two batches to avoid overcrowding the pan, and cook for 5 minutes on each side, or until well browned. Drain on kitchen paper and serve hot.

STARTERS & SIDES

VEGETABLE PAKORAS

Makes: 4   **Prep: 25 mins**   **Cook: 20–25 mins**

Ingredients

6 tbsp gram flour

½ tsp salt

1 tsp chilli powder

1 tsp baking powder

1½ tsp white cumin seeds

1 tsp pomegranate seeds

300 ml/10 fl oz water

2 tbsp chopped fresh coriander, plus extra sprigs, to garnish

vegetables of your choice: cauliflower, cut into small florets; onions, cut into rings; potatoes, sliced; aubergines, sliced; or fresh spinach leaves

vegetable or groundnut oil, for deep-frying

Method

1 Sift the gram flour into a large bowl. Add the salt, chilli and baking powders, cumin and pomegranate seeds and blend together well. Pour in the water and beat well to form a smooth batter. Add the chopped coriander and mix well, then set aside.

2 Heat enough oil for deep-frying in a large, heavy-based saucepan or a deep-fryer until it reaches 180–190°C/350–375°F or until a cube of bread browns in 30 seconds.

3 Dip the prepared vegetables into the batter, carefully shaking off any excess. Using tongs, place them in the oil and deep-fry in batches, turning once.

4 Repeat this process until all of the batter and vegetables have been used up. Transfer the battered vegetables to kitchen paper and drain thoroughly. Garnish with coriander sprigs and serve immediately.

FISH PAKORAS

Serves: 4

Prep: 25 mins, plus standing

Cook: 20–25 mins

Ingredients

½ tsp salt

2 tbsp lemon juice

700 g/1 lb 9 oz skinless white fish, such as cod or halibut

vegetable or groundnut oil, for deep-frying

pepper, to taste

lemon wedges, to serve

Batter

140 g/5 oz gram flour

seeds from 4 green cardamom pods

pinch of ground turmeric

large pinch of bicarbonate of soda

finely grated rind of 1 lemon

175 ml/6 fl oz water

salt and pepper

Method

1 Combine the salt, lemon juice and pepper to taste in a small bowl. Rinse and dry the fish fillets, then cut into large chunks and rub the marinade all over the fish. Leave to stand for 20–30 minutes.

2 To make the batter, put the gram flour in a bowl and stir in the cardamom seeds, turmeric, bicarbonate of soda, lemon rind, and salt and pepper to taste. Make a well in the centre and gradually stir in the water until a thin batter forms. Gently stir the pieces of fish into the batter to coat.

3 Heat enough oil for deep-frying in a large, heavy-based saucepan or a deep-fryer to 180–190°C/350–375°F or until a cube of bread browns in 30 seconds. Remove the fish pieces from the batter, carefully shaking off any excess. Without overcrowding the pan, drop the fish pieces in the oil and fry for 2½–3 minutes, or until golden brown.

4 Use a slotted spoon to remove the fish pieces and drain on kitchen paper. Continue until all the fish is fried, then serve hot with the lemon wedges.

STARTERS & SIDES

ONION BHAJIS

Serves: 4   **Prep: 15 mins**   **Cook: 30 mins**

Ingredients

150 g/5½ oz gram flour

1 tsp salt, or to taste

small pinch of bicarbonate of soda

25 g/1 oz ground rice

1 tsp fennel seeds

1 tsp cumin seeds

2 fresh green chillies, finely chopped

2 large onions, sliced into half-rings and separated

1 tbsp chopped fresh coriander

200 ml/7 fl oz cold water

vegetable or groundnut oil, for deep-frying

Method

1 Sift the gram flour into a large bowl and add the salt, bicarbonate of soda, ground rice, fennel and cumin seeds. Mix together well, then add the chillies, onions and coriander. Gradually pour in the water and mix until a thick batter forms and the onions are thoroughly coated.

2 Heat enough oil for deep-frying in a large, heavy-based saucepan or deep-fryer to 180–190°C/350–375°F or until a cube of bread browns in 30 seconds. Add the onion batter, ½ a teaspoon at a time, to the hot oil, being careful not to overcrowd the pan. Reduce the heat slightly and cook the fritters for 8–10 minutes, until golden brown and crisp.

3 Use a slotted spoon to remove the fritters and drain on kitchen paper. Continue until all the batter mixture has been used. Serve hot.

STARTERS & SIDES

STUFFED CHILLI BHAJIS

Serves: 4

Prep: 25 mins, plus soaking

Cook: 15–20 mins

Ingredients

8 large fresh green chillies

vegetable or groundnut oil, for deep-frying

chutney, to serve

Batter

250 g/9 oz gram flour

125 g/4½ oz rice flour

½ tsp baking powder

1 tsp ground cumin

2 tsp salt

1 tsp chilli powder

about 700 ml/1¼ pints cold water

Stuffing

2 tbsp vegetable or groundnut oil

1 tsp fennel seeds

2 tsp black mustard seeds

1 tsp cumin seeds

1 potato, boiled and mashed

3 tbsp finely chopped fresh coriander

1 tsp salt

½ tsp tamarind paste

1 tbsp roasted peanuts, roughly chopped

Method

1 Slit the chillies lengthways and remove the seeds using a small teaspoon. Soak the chillies in boiling water for 5 minutes. Drain on kitchen paper and set aside.

2 Mix together all the batter ingredients in a bowl, adding enough of the water to make a thin batter the consistency of double cream. Set aside.

3 For the stuffing, heat the oil in a frying pan and add the fennel, mustard and cumin seeds. When the seeds start to pop, add the potato, coriander and salt, and mix well. Add the tamarind paste and sprinkle over the roasted peanuts. Remove from the heat and mash until evenly combined.

4 Using your fingers, stuff the green chillies with the potato mixture.

5 Heat enough oil for deep-frying in a large, heavy-based saucepan or deep-fryer to 180–190°C/350–375°F or until a cube of bread browns in 30 seconds. Working in batches, dip the stuffed green chillies in the batter and deep-fry, for 2–3 minutes, or until crisp and golden. Remove with a slotted spoon and drain on kitchen paper. Serve warm with chutney for dipping.

STARTERS & SIDES

PANEER TIKKA

Serves: 4

Prep: 25 mins, plus marinating or chilling

Cook: 15–20 mins

Ingredients

350 g/12 oz paneer, cut into 16 cubes

vegetable or groundnut oil, for brushing

1 tsp garam masala

fresh coriander leaves, to garnish

Tikka paste

10 black peppercorns

6 cloves

seeds from 4 green cardamom pods

1 tsp cumin seeds

1 tsp coriander seeds

½ tsp poppy seeds

½ tsp chilli powder

½ tsp ground turmeric

1 tbsp garlic paste

1 tbsp ginger paste

½ small onion, chopped

150 g/5½ oz natural yogurt

½ tbsp tomato purée

1 tbsp gram flour

1 tbsp vegetable or groundnut oil

Method

1 To make the tikka paste, dry-fry the peppercorns cloves, cardamom, cumin, coriander and poppy seeds in a frying pan over a high heat, stirring constantly, until they release their aroma. Immediately tip out of the pan so they don't burn.

2 Put the spices in a spice grinder or mortar. Add the chilli powder and turmeric, and grind to a fine powder. Add the garlic and ginger pastes and onion, and continue grinding until a paste forms. Transfer to a large bowl and stir in the yogurt, tomato purée, gram flour and oil.

3 Add the paneer to the bowl and use your hands to coat the cubes in the tikka paste, taking care not to break up the pieces of cheese. Cover and leave to marinate at room temperature for 30 minutes, or chill for up to 24 hours.

4 Preheat the grill to medium–high. If you have refrigerated the cheese, remove it from the refrigerator 15 minutes before cooking. Lightly brush four metal skewers with oil. Drain the paneer and thread four pieces onto each of the skewers, leaving a little space between each cube.

5 Cook the skewers under the preheated grill for 12–15 minutes, turning once and basting with any remaining tikka paste, until the paneer is lightly charred.

6 To serve, sprinkle the hot kebabs with the garam masala and garnish with coriander leaves.

TAPIOCA & POTATO CAKES

Makes: 15–20   **Prep: 20 mins**   **Cook: 35–40 mins**

Ingredients

2 potatoes, roughly chopped

200 g/7 oz medium-sized tapioca pearls

250 ml/9 fl oz cold water

2 fresh red chillies, finely chopped

1 tsp cumin seeds

1 tsp salt

4 tbsp finely chopped fresh coriander

vegetable or groundnut oil, for deep-frying

Method

1 Place the potatoes in a saucepan of boiling water and cook for 12–15 minutes, or until just tender. Drain thoroughly and transfer to a mixing bowl.

2 Meanwhile, place the tapioca in another bowl and pour over the cold water. Leave to soak for 12–15 minutes, or until the water has been absorbed and the tapioca is swollen. Transfer to a sieve and drain any excess liquid.

3 Add the chillies, cumin seeds, salt and coriander to the potatoes and mash until fairly smooth. Stir in the soaked tapioca and mix well. With wet hands, roll the mixture into 15–20 walnut-sized balls, then flatten each to make patties.

4 Heat enough oil for deep-frying in a large, heavy-based saucepan or deep-fryer to 180–190°C/350–375°F or until a cube of bread browns in 30 seconds. Working in batches, deep-fry the tapioca and potato cakes, for 3–4 minutes, or until golden brown. Remove with a slotted spoon and drain on kitchen paper. Serve warm.

SPICED GRAM FLOUR ROLLS

Serves: 6　　　　**Prep: 30 mins**　　　　**Cook: 15–20 mins,** plus standing

Ingredients

vegetable or groundnut oil, for greasing

250 g/9 oz gram flour, sifted

100 g/3½ oz natural yogurt

600 ml/1 pint warm water

2 tsp salt

¼ tsp ground turmeric

2 tsp grated fresh ginger

2 garlic cloves, crushed

4 tsp green chilli paste

Topping

6 tbsp vegetable or groundnut oil

1 tsp sesame seeds

1 tsp black mustard seeds

4 tbsp finely chopped fresh coriander

2 tbsp freshly grated coconut

Method

1 Lightly brush four large baking trays with oil and set aside.

2 Combine the gram flour, yogurt, water, salt, turmeric, ginger, garlic and green chilli paste in a large, heavy-based saucepan. Whisk until smooth, then place over a medium heat and continue to whisk constantly. When the batter starts to thicken (after about 5–6 minutes), reduce the heat to low, cover and cook for 4–5 minutes. Stir, re-cover and cook for a further 2–3 minutes, or until thickened and smooth.

3 Remove from the heat and ladle the batter onto the prepared baking trays, using a palette knife to spread the mixture as thinly as possible. The batter will start to set as it cools. Leave to stand for 5 minutes, then slice it lengthways into 5-cm/2-inch wide strips.

4 Starting at one end of each strip, use the palette knife to gently lift and roll (like a small Swiss roll). Repeat until all the strips have been rolled. Transfer to a serving plate.

5 Meanwhile, make the topping. Heat the oil in a frying pan and add the sesame and mustard seeds. When they start to pop, remove from the heat and drizzle over the gram flour rolls. Sprinkle over the coriander and coconut and serve.

STARTERS & SIDES

CRISPY CHILLI SQUID

Serves: 4

Prep: 20 mins, plus marinating

Cook: 15–20 mins

Ingredients

500 g/1 lb 2 oz prepared squid rings

5 tbsp semolina

6 tbsp cornflour

vegetable or groundnut oil, for deep-frying

Marinade

3 fresh red chillies, finely chopped

2 tsp finely grated fresh ginger

3 garlic cloves, crushed

2 tbsp white wine vinegar

4 tbsp vegetable or groundnut oil

1 tsp ground cumin

1 tsp coriander seeds, lightly crushed

1 tsp salt

Method

1 Place all the marinade ingredients in a small food processor and process until smooth. Transfer to a shallow dish and add the squid rings. Toss to mix well, cover and leave to marinate in the refrigerator for 1 hour.

2 In a separate bowl, mix together the semolina and cornflour. Set aside.

3 Heat enough oil for deep-frying in a large, heavy-based saucepan or deep-fryer to 180–190°C/350–375°F or until a cube of bread browns in 30 seconds. Remove the squid from its marinade and toss it in the semolina mixture to coat. Shake off any excess and deep-fry the squid in batches, for 1–2 minutes, or until crisp and golden.

4 Remove the squid with a slotted spoon and drain on kitchen paper. Serve immediately.

MASALA PRAWN CAKES

Makes: 20

Prep: 25 mins, plus chilling

Cook: 12–15 mins

Ingredients

4 tbsp vegetable or groundnut oil

lime wedges, to serve

Prawn cakes

800 g/1 lb 12 oz raw tiger prawns, peeled and deveined

2 fresh red chillies, deseeded and very finely chopped

6 tbsp finely chopped fresh coriander

6 tbsp finely chopped fresh mint

1 tsp coconut cream

4 spring onions, finely sliced

2 garlic cloves, finely chopped

2 tsp finely grated fresh ginger

8 tbsp fresh white breadcrumbs

2 tsp ground cumin

1 tsp chilli powder

1 small egg, lightly beaten

Method

1 To make the prawn cakes, roughly chop the prawns and place them in a food processor with the remaining ingredients. Process to a coarse paste. Transfer the mixture to a bowl, cover and chill in the refrigerator for at least 6–8 hours, or overnight.

2 Preheat the oven to 200°C/400°F/Gas Mark 6. Line a baking tray with baking paper.

3 Shape the prawn mixture into 20 small cakes, approximately 4 cm/1½ inches in diameter. Place on the prepared baking tray and lightly brush with the oil. Bake in the preheated oven for 12–15 minutes, or until slightly puffed up and light golden.

4 Serve warm or at room temperature with lime wedges for squeezing over.

GARLIC PRAWNS

Serves: 4   **Prep: 10 mins**   **Cook: 12 mins**

Ingredients

175 g/6 oz butter

8 large garlic cloves, finely chopped

1 kg/2 lb 4 oz cooked prawns, unpeeled

large handful of fresh flat-leaf parsley, finely chopped

salt and pepper

Method

1 Set a very large frying pan or large, heavy-based saucepan over a low heat and add the butter. When the butter has melted add the garlic and cook gently, stirring occasionally, for 5 minutes.

2 Once the garlic begins to brown, add the prawns and gently stir them through the butter. Increase the heat to medium, cover and cook, shaking the pan occasionally, for 3 minutes. Add the parsley and cook for a further 2 minutes. Add plenty of salt and pepper and transfer to a large serving bowl.

3 Place in the middle of the table with another bowl for the prawn shells. Serve immediately.

SPICY CHICKEN SKEWERS

Serves: 4

Prep: 20 mins, plus soaking

Cook: 8–10 mins

Ingredients

500 g/1 lb 2 oz skinless, boneless chicken breasts

3 tbsp tomato purée

2 tbsp clear honey

2 tbsp Worcestershire sauce

1 tbsp chopped fresh rosemary

250 g/9 oz cherry tomatoes

fresh rosemary sprigs, to garnish

freshly cooked couscous or rice, to serve

Method

1. Using a sharp knife, cut the chicken into 2.5-cm/1-inch chunks and place in a bowl. Mix together the tomato purée, honey, Worcestershire sauce and rosemary in a separate bowl, then add to the chicken, stirring to coat evenly.

2. Soak eight wooden skewers in a bowl of cold water for 30 minutes to prevent them burning during cooking. Preheat the grill to hot. Thread the chicken pieces and cherry tomatoes alternately onto the skewers and place them on a grill rack.

3. Spoon over any remaining glaze and cook under the preheated grill for 8–10 minutes, turning occasionally, until the chicken is cooked through. Transfer to four large serving plates and serve with freshly cooked couscous or rice. Garnish with a few sprigs of fresh rosemary.

STARTERS & SIDES

STEAMED CHICKEN DUMPLINGS

Makes: 20

Prep: 35 mins,
plus marinating & resting

Cook: 12–15 mins

Ingredients

1 tbsp white wine vinegar

1 tbsp dark soy sauce

6 spring onions,
very finely chopped

2 garlic cloves, crushed

2 tsp salt

2 fresh green chillies,
finely chopped

200 g/7 oz chicken mince

150 g/5½ oz plain flour,
plus extra for dusting

5 tbsp tepid water

2 tbsp vegetable or
groundnut oil, plus extra
for brushing

sweet chilli sauce, to serve

Method

1 Mix together the vinegar, soy sauce, spring onions, garlic, 1 teaspoon of the salt and the chillies in a bowl. Add the chicken mince and, using your fingers, mix until well combined. Cover and leave to marinate for 30 minutes.

2 Meanwhile, sift the flour and the remaining salt into another large bowl. Add the water and oil and knead for 8–10 minutes to make a soft dough. Cover and leave to rest for 15–20 minutes.

3 Divide the dough into 20 small balls. On a lightly floured surface, roll out each ball into a thin 10-cm/4-inch round.

4 Place a little of the chicken mixture in the centre of each dough round. Fold the dough in half to make a semi-circular dumpling, sealing it tightly by carefully pinching the folded edges together.

5 Place the dumplings in a single layer in a steamer and lightly brush with oil. Steam over a high heat for 12–15 minutes, or until the chicken is cooked through. Serve warm with sweet chilli sauce.

STARTERS & SIDES

FIRECRACKER CHICKEN WITH PLUM & ORANGE SAUCE

Serves: 4   **Prep: 20 mins**   **Cook: 35–37 mins**

Ingredients

1 kg/2 lb 4 oz chicken wings or legs

500 ml/18 fl oz water

3 tbsp vegetable or groundnut oil

1 tbsp toasted sesame oil

1 small red pepper, finely diced

2 garlic cloves, finely chopped

2.5-cm/1-inch piece fresh ginger, very finely chopped

5 spring onions, chopped

55 g/2 oz fresh coriander, chopped

1 tbsp crushed red chilli flakes

2 tbsp rice vinegar or white wine vinegar

finely grated rind of 1 small orange

½ tsp salt

½ tsp pepper

200 g/7 oz plum sauce

1 tbsp sesame seeds

Method

1 Discard the chicken wing tips, then cut the wings in two at the joint. Bring the water to the boil in a large wok fitted with a rack and a lid. Spread the chicken on the rack in a single layer and place in the wok. (If your wok does not have a rack, use a saucepan and a steamer basket.) Steam for 15 minutes, until the juices run clear when a skewer is inserted into the thickest part of the meat.

2 Blot the chicken with kitchen paper and tip into a dish. Add the groundnut oil and sesame oil to the wok and heat until very hot. Add the red pepper, garlic, ginger and spring onions, and stir-fry over a medium–high heat for 2 minutes. Stir in the coriander, chilli flakes, vinegar, orange rind, salt and pepper, and stir-fry for a further minute. Add the plum sauce and bubble for 2 minutes, stirring vigorously.

3 Add the chicken and stir-fry for 8–10 minutes, until the liquid has almost evaporated and the sauce has started to coat the meat. Add the sesame seeds and stir-fry for a further minute, or until the chicken is golden and glazed. Transfer to warm bowls to serve.

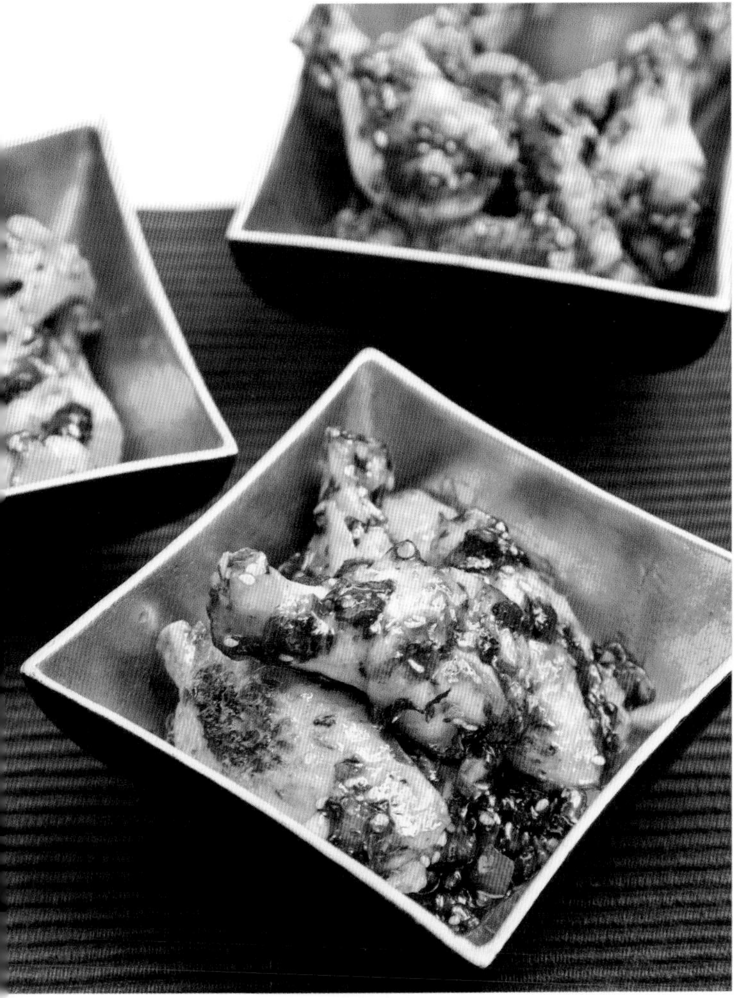

CHICKEN & EGG ROLLS

Makes: 6

Prep: 30 mins, plus chilling & resting

Cook: 25–30 mins

Ingredients

2 skinless, boneless chicken breasts, cut into bite-sized pieces

200 g/7 oz plain flour, plus extra for dusting

1 tsp salt

1 tbsp vegetable or groundnut oil

100 ml/3½ fl oz milk

4 eggs

fresh mint and sliced red onion, to serve

Marinade

2 garlic cloves, crushed

1 tsp grated fresh ginger

2 tsp ground cumin

1 tsp chilli powder

¼ tsp ground turmeric

¼ tsp garam masala

2 tsp tomato purée

2 tbsp natural yogurt

1 tbsp lemon juice

1 tsp salt

1 tbsp vegetable or groundnut oil

Method

1 Place all the marinade ingredients in a bowl with the chicken and stir to mix well. Cover and chill in the refrigerator for 6–8 hours or overnight. When ready to cook, preheat the grill to medium–high. Thread the marinated chicken onto metal skewers and cook under the preheated grill, turning once, for 12–15 minutes, until cooked through. Remove the chicken from the skewers and keep warm.

2 Meanwhile, sift the flour and salt into a large bowl. Add the oil, milk and one of the eggs and knead for 8–10 minutes, until smooth. Form into a ball, cover and leave to rest for 15–20 minutes. Divide the dough into six equal-sized pieces and form each into a ball. On a lightly floured surface, roll each ball into a 16-cm/6¼-inch round. Lightly beat the remaining eggs.

3 Heat a non-stick frying pan over a medium heat. One at a time, place a dough round in the pan and cook for 1 minute. Flip it over and spread 1 tablespoon of the beaten egg over the surface. Immediately flip it over again and cook for 30–40 seconds, then remove from the heat. Repeat until all the dough has been cooked.

4 Divide the chicken between the egg rolls and scatter over the mint and red onion. Roll tightly to enclose the filling and serve immediately.

STARTERS & SIDES

SPICED POTATO & VEGETABLE SNACK

Serves: 4   **Prep: 20 mins**   **Cook: 50–60 mins**

Ingredients

4 tbsp vegetable or groundnut oil

50 g/1¾ oz butter

2 garlic cloves, crushed

2 fresh green chillies, finely chopped

1 large onion, finely chopped

2 tsp grated fresh ginger

400 g/14 oz canned chopped tomatoes

200 g/7 oz cauliflower, finely chopped

100 g/3½ oz green cabbage, finely chopped

200 g/7 oz fresh shelled or frozen peas

1 large carrot, coarsely grated

4 potatoes, boiled and mashed

3 tbsp pao bhaji masala

2 tsp salt

1 tbsp lemon juice

4 tbsp finely chopped fresh coriander

4 white rolls, to serve

Method

1 Heat the oil and butter in a wok or large frying pan over a medium heat. Sauté the garlic and chillies for 30 seconds, then stir in the onion and ginger. Stir-fry for 8–10 minutes, or until the onion is lightly browned.

2 Add the tomatoes and stir-fry for 6–8 minutes, or until thickened. Stir in the cauliflower, cabbage, peas, carrot and potatoes. Add the pao bhaji masala. Cover and cook, stirring occasionally, for 15–20 minutes.

3 Preheat the grill. Season the potato and vegetable mixture with the salt and stir in the lemon juice. Remove from the heat and scatter over the chopped coriander. Split the rolls in half and lightly toast them under the preheated grill. Serve the potato mixture in warmed bowls with the toasted rolls.

BOMBAY POTATOES

Serves: 4   **Prep: 15 mins**   **Cook: 1¼ hours**

Ingredients

1 kg/2 lb 4 oz waxy potatoes

2 tbsp ghee

1 tsp panch phoran spice mix

3 tsp ground turmeric

2 tbsp tomato purée

300 ml/10 fl oz natural yogurt

salt

1 tbsp chopped fresh coriander, to garnish

Method

1 Preheat the oven to 180°C/350°F/Gas Mark 4. Put the whole potatoes into a large saucepan of salted cold water. Bring to the boil, then simmer for about 15 minutes, until the potatoes are just cooked, but not soft.

2 Heat the ghee in a separate saucepan over a medium heat and add the panch phoran, turmeric, tomato purée, yogurt and salt. Bring to the boil and simmer, uncovered, for 5 minutes.

3 Drain the potatoes and cut each one into four pieces. Add the potatoes to the pan, then cover and cook for 5 minutes. Transfer to an ovenproof dish. Place in the oven and cook for 40 minutes, or until the potatoes are tender and the sauce has thickened a little. Sprinkle with chopped coriander and serve immediately.

★ Variation

Try replacing the potato with cauliflower – it has a much lighter texture, absorbs flavour well and holds its shape during cooking.

VEGETABLES & PULSES

VEGETABLE KORMA

Serves: 4

Prep: 15 mins, plus soaking

Cook: 55–60 mins

Ingredients

85 g/3 oz cashew nuts

175 ml/6 fl oz boiling water

good pinch of saffron threads, pounded

2 tbsp hot milk

1 small cauliflower, divided into 1-cm/½-inch florets

115 g/4 oz French beans, cut into 2.5-cm/1-inch lengths

115 g/4 oz carrots, cut into 2.5-cm/1-inch sticks

250 g/9 oz new potatoes, boiled in their skins and cooled

4 tbsp sunflower oil

1 large onion, finely chopped

2 tsp ginger purée

1–2 fresh green chillies, chopped

2 tsp ground coriander

½ tsp ground turmeric

6 tbsp lukewarm water

400 ml/14 fl oz vegetable stock

½ tsp salt, or to taste

2 tbsp single cream

2 tsp ghee or butter

1 tsp garam masala

¼ tsp grated nutmeg

Method

1 Place the cashew nuts in a heatproof bowl with the boiling water and soak for 20 minutes. Meanwhile, place the saffron in a small bowl with the milk and leave to soak.

2 Bring a saucepan of lightly salted water to the boil and blanch the vegetables separately, for 3–4 minutes each (the potatoes might take a little longer), then drain and plunge into cold water. Once boiled, peel the potatoes if you like, and halve or quarter them according to their size.

3 Heat a medium-sized, heavy-based saucepan over a medium heat, then add the oil. Add the onion, ginger purée and chillies and cook, stirring frequently, for 5–6 minutes, until the onion is soft. Add the coriander and turmeric and cook, stirring, for a further minute. Add 3 tablespoons of the water and cook for 2–3 minutes. Add the remaining water, then cook, stirring frequently, for 2–3 minutes, or until the oil separates from the spice paste.

4 Add the stock, saffron and milk mixture, and salt, then bring to the boil. Drain the vegetables, add to the saucepan and return to the boil. Reduce the heat to low and simmer for 2–3 minutes. Meanwhile, put the cashew nuts and their

VEGETABLES & PULSES

soaking water in a food processor and process to a thick paste. Add to the korma, then stir in the cream. Leave to cook over a very low heat while you prepare the final seasoning.

5 Heat a very small saucepan over a low heat, then add the ghee. Add the garam masala and nutmeg and leave the spices to sizzle gently for 20–25 seconds. Fold the spiced butter into the korma. Remove from the heat and serve immediately.

★ Variation

This delicious korma sauce can be used with any vegetables – try mixing with some wilted spinach and steamed tenderstem broccoli for a side dish.

BENGALI VEGETABLE CURRY

Serves: 4

Prep: 25 mins, plus soaking

Cook: 30–35 mins

Ingredients

6 tbsp white poppy seeds (khus khus)

3 tbsp black mustard seeds

2 tsp grated fresh ginger

4 tbsp vegetable or groundnut oil

2 fresh green chillies, split lengthways

1 tbsp panch phoran spice mix

200 g/7 oz fresh bittergourd (kerala), cut into 1.5-cm/⅝-inch cubes

2 potatoes, cut into 1.5-cm/⅝-inch cubes

1 aubergine, cut into 1.5-cm/⅝-inch cubes

1 courgette, cut into 1.5-cm/⅝-inch cubes

1 carrot, cut into 1.5-cm/⅝-inch cubes

1 tomato, finely chopped

100 g/3½ oz fresh or frozen peas

400 ml/14 fl oz cold water

¼ tsp ground turmeric

2 tsp salt

1 tsp palm sugar

125 ml/4 fl oz milk

Method

1 Soak the white poppy seeds and 2 tablespoons of the mustard seeds in warm water for 1 hour. Drain and blend with the ginger to make a paste.

2 Heat the oil in a wok or large frying pan and add the remaining mustard seeds and the chillies. When the mustard seeds start to pop, add the panch phoran and all the vegetables. Add half the water and stir to mix well, then cover tightly and cook, stirring frequently, over a medium heat for 10–12 minutes.

3 Add half the white poppy and mustard seed paste, the turmeric and salt. Add the remaining water and cook, stirring frequently, over a low–medium heat for a further 10–15 minutes.

4 Add the remaining white poppy and mustard seed paste, the palm sugar and milk, and cook for a further 5 minutes, or until the vegetables are tender. Serve hot.

VEGETABLES & PULSES

AUBERGINE & BEAN CURRY

Serves: 4   **Prep: 10 mins**   **Cook: 12–15 mins**

Ingredients

2 tbsp vegetable or groundnut oil

1 onion, finely chopped

2 garlic cloves, crushed

2 fresh red chillies, deseeded and chopped

1 tbsp red curry paste

1 large aubergine, cut into large chunks

115 g/4 oz baby aubergines

115 g/4 oz baby broad beans

115 g/4 oz French beans

300 ml/10 fl oz vegetable stock

55 g/2 oz block creamed coconut, chopped

3 tbsp soy sauce

1 tsp soft light brown sugar

3 kaffir lime leaves, torn coarsely

4 tbsp chopped fresh coriander, to garnish

Method

1 Heat a wok or large, heavy-based saucepan over a medium–high heat and add the oil. Fry the onion, garlic and chillies for 1–2 minutes. Stir in the curry paste and cook for 1–2 minutes.

2 Add all the aubergines and cook for 3–4 minutes until starting to soften. (You may need to add a little more oil as aubergines soak it up quickly.) Add the beans and fry, stirring constantly, for 2 minutes.

3 Pour in the stock and add the creamed coconut, soy sauce, sugar and lime leaves. Bring gently to the boil and cook until the coconut has dissolved. Sprinkle over the coriander and serve hot.

TANDOORI MUSHROOM CURRY

Serves: 4   **Prep: 15 mins**   **Cook: 35–40 mins**

Ingredients

2 tbsp vegetable or groundnut oil

1 tsp cumin seeds

1 tsp coriander seeds

1 onion, finely chopped

2 tsp ground coriander

1 tsp ground cumin

6 black peppercorns

½ tsp freshly ground cardamom seeds

1 tsp ground turmeric

1 tbsp tandoori masala

1 fresh red chilli, finely chopped

2 garlic cloves, crushed

2 tsp grated fresh ginger

800 g/1 lb 12 oz canned chopped tomatoes

600 g/1 lb 5 oz chestnut or button mushrooms, halved

2 tsp salt

200 g/7 oz fresh or frozen peas

4 tbsp chopped fresh coriander

6 tbsp single cream

chapatis, to serve

Method

1. Heat the oil in a large, heavy-based saucepan over a medium heat. Add the cumin and coriander seeds and cook for 1 minute, or until sizzling.

2. Add the onion, ground coriander, cumin, peppercorns, ground cardamom seeds, turmeric, tandoori masala, chilli, garlic and ginger. Cook, stirring, for 2–3 minutes, or until the onion is soft and the spices have released their aroma.

3. Add the tomatoes, mushrooms and salt. Stir until well combined. Bring to the boil, then reduce the heat to low and cook, uncovered, for 25 minutes.

4. Add the peas and stir to mix well. Cook for a further 4–5 minutes, or until piping hot.

5. Remove from the heat, scatter over the coriander and drizzle over the cream. Stir to mix well and serve immediately with chapatis.

RED CURRY WITH MIXED LEAVES

Serves: 4   **Prep: 15 mins**   **Cook: 8-12 mins**

Ingredients

2 tbsp vegetable or groundnut oil

2 onions, thinly sliced

bunch of fine asparagus spears

400 ml/14 fl oz coconut milk

2 tbsp red curry paste

3 fresh kaffir lime leaves

225 g/8 oz baby spinach leaves

2 heads bok choi, chopped

1 small head Chinese leaves, shredded

handful of fresh coriander, chopped

cooked rice, to serve

Method

1 Heat a wok or large, heavy-based saucepan over a medium–high heat and add the oil. Add the onions and asparagus and fry, stirring constantly, for 1–2 minutes.

2 Add the coconut milk, curry paste and lime leaves and bring gently to the boil, stirring occasionally.

3 Add the spinach, bok choi and Chinese leaves and cook, stirring, for 2–3 minutes, until the greens have wilted. Add the coriander and stir well. Serve immediately with freshly cooked rice.

SOUTH INDIAN LENTIL & VEGETABLE CURRY

Serves: 4–6

Prep: 20 mins, plus soaking

Cook: 25–30 mins

Ingredients

250 g/9 oz split red lentils (masoor dhal), rinsed

175 g/6 oz new potatoes, finely diced

1 large carrot, finely diced

1 green pepper, finely chopped

1 litre/1¾ pints cold water

¼ tsp ground turmeric

¼ tsp asafoetida

1 tbsp tamarind paste

2 tsp sambhar masala, or to taste

salt, to taste

Garnish

1½ tbsp vegetable oil

12 fresh curry leaves

1 tsp black mustard seeds

Method

1. Put the red lentils in a bowl with enough water to cover and leave to soak for 30 minutes, changing the water once.

2. Drain the lentils. Put them in a large frying pan with the potatoes, carrot and green pepper, and pour over the water. Bring to the boil, skimming the surface as necessary. Reduce the heat to its lowest setting, stir in the turmeric and asafoetida and partially cover the pan. Simmer, stirring occasionally, for 15–20 minutes, until the vegetables and lentils are tender but not soft.

3. Stir in the tamarind paste and sambhar masala. Taste and adjust the seasoning, adding extra masala and salt if necessary. Leave to simmer gently while you prepare the garnish.

4. To make the garnish, heat the oil in a large frying pan over a high heat. Add the curry leaves and mustard seeds and stir quickly, taking care to stand back as they will pop. Transfer the lentil mixture to a serving dish and pour over the hot oil and spices. Serve immediately.

CHICKPEA CURRY

Serves: 4　　　　**Prep: 15 mins**　　　　**Cook: 18–20 mins**

Ingredients

6 tbsp vegetable or
groundnut oil

2 onions, sliced

1 tsp finely chopped
fresh ginger

1 tsp ground cumin

1 tsp ground coriander

1 tsp crushed fresh garlic

1 tsp chilli powder

2 fresh green chillies,
finely chopped

2–3 tbsp chopped
fresh coriander

150 ml/5 fl oz water

1 large potato

400 g/14 oz canned
chickpeas, drained

1 tbsp lemon juice

Method

1 Heat the oil in a large, heavy-based saucepan. Add the onions and cook, stirring occasionally, until golden. Reduce the heat, add the ginger, ground cumin and coriander, garlic, chilli powder, green chillies and coriander leaves and fry, stirring constantly, for 2 minutes. Add the water to the saucepan and stir to mix.

2 Using a sharp knife, cut the potato into dice, then add to the saucepan with the chickpeas. Cover and leave to simmer, stirring occasionally, for 5–7 minutes.

3 Sprinkle the lemon juice over the curry. Transfer to warmed serving dishes and serve hot.

VEGETABLES & PULSES

KASHMIRI VEGETABLES

Serves: 4   **Prep: 15 mins**   **Cook: 35 mins**

Ingredients

3 tbsp ghee or vegetable oil

2 tbsp flaked almonds

seeds from 8 cardamom pods

8 black peppercorns

2 tsp cumin seeds

1 cinnamon stick

2 fresh green chillies, deseeded and chopped

1 tsp ginger paste

1 tsp chilli powder

3 potatoes, cut into chunks

225 g/8 oz okra, cut into 2.5-cm/1-inch pieces

½ cauliflower, broken into florets

150 ml/5 fl oz natural yogurt

150 ml/5 fl oz vegetable stock or water

salt, to taste

cooked rice, to serve

Method

1 Heat 1 tablespoon of the ghee in a large, heavy-based saucepan. Add the almonds and cook over a low heat, stirring constantly, for 2 minutes, or until golden.

2 Remove the almonds from the saucepan with a slotted spoon, drain on kitchen paper and set aside. Place the cardamom seeds, peppercorns, cumin seeds and cinnamon stick in a spice grinder or mortar, and grind finely.

3 Add the remaining ghee to the saucepan and heat. Add the green chillies and cook, stirring frequently, for 2 minutes. Stir in the ginger paste, chilli powder and ground spices and cook, stirring constantly, for 2 minutes, or until they release their aroma.

4 Add the potatoes, season with salt. Cover and cook, stirring occasionally, for 8 minutes. Add the okra and cauliflower and cook for a further 5 minutes.

5 Gradually stir in the yogurt and stock and bring to the boil. Cover and simmer for a further 10 minutes, until all the vegetables are tender. Garnish with the reserved flaked almonds and serve with freshly cooked rice.

SPICED AUBERGINE MASH

Serves: 4

Prep: 20 mins, plus cooling

Cook: 45–55 mins

Ingredients

4 large aubergines

2 tbsp vegetable or groundnut oil

55 g/2 oz butter

2 onions, finely chopped

2 tsp grated fresh ginger

4 garlic cloves, crushed

2 fresh green chillies, finely sliced

3 tomatoes, finely chopped

2 tsp salt

1 tsp chilli powder

1 tsp smoked paprika

2 tsp ground coriander

1 tsp ground cumin

1 tsp ground turmeric

½ tsp garam masala

6 tbsp finely chopped fresh coriander

Method

1 Prick the aubergines all over with a fork and roast them over an open flame (if you have a gas hob) or under a medium–hot grill, turning them from time to time, for 20–25 minutes, until the skin blackens and chars. To check if the aubergines are cooked, press the back of a spoon into the skin – if it gives like soft butter, it is done. Allow to cool.

2 When the aubergines are cool enough to handle, remove the skins and roughly mash the flesh. Set aside.

3 Heat the oil and butter in a large frying pan and add the onions. Sauté for 5–6 minutes, until softened. Add the ginger, garlic and chillies and stir-fry for 1–2 minutes.

4 Stir in the tomatoes and salt and cook for 12–15 minutes. Add the chilli powder, paprika, ground coriander, cumin and turmeric.

5 Stir in the reserved aubergine flesh and cook for about 3–4 minutes. Stir in the garam masala and chopped coriander. Serve immediately.

TOMATO-STUFFED AUBERGINES

Makes: 4　　　　**Prep: 35 mins**　　　　**Cook: 30–35 mins**

Ingredients

4 small aubergines, about
13 cm/5 inches long

vegetable or groundnut oil,
for shallow-frying

natural yogurt, to serve

mint sprigs, to garnish

Stuffing

4 firm tomatoes, grated

2 onions, grated

2 fresh red chillies, chopped

4 tbsp lemon juice

4 tbsp finely chopped
fresh coriander

½ tbsp garlic paste

½ tbsp ginger paste

1½ tbsp ground coriander

2 tsp ground cumin

1 tsp fennel seeds

1 tsp ground turmeric

1 tsp salt

1 tbsp gram flour
(if needed)

naan bread, to serve

Method

1　To make the stuffing, mix together the tomatoes, onions, chillies, lemon juice, chopped coriander, garlic and ginger pastes, ground coriander and cumin, fennel seeds, turmeric and salt in a bowl. The stuffing should not be stiff, but thick enough that it doesn't slide off the aubergine slices. If the tomatoes are very juicy and have made the filling too runny, gradually stir in the gram flour.

2　To prepare the aubergines, work one at a time. Slit lengthways into four parallel slices, without cutting through the stem end, so that the aubergine remains in one piece. Lightly fan the slices apart, then use a small spoon to spread a quarter of the stuffing over the slices, covering each slice to the edges. Carefully layer the slices back into position so the aubergine looks whole again. Repeat this process with the remaining aubergines.

3　Choose a heavy-based frying pan with a tight-fitting lid – it needs to be large enough to hold the aubergines in a single layer. Heat enough oil to cover the base of the pan to about 5 mm/¼ inch deep, then add the aubergines in a single layer.

4 Put the pan over the lowest heat and cover tightly. Leave to cook for
15 minutes, then carefully turn the aubergines over. Re-cover the pan
and continue cooking for a further 10–15 minutes, or until the aubergines
are tender when you pierce them with a skewer or a knife. Serve hot with
naan bread.

SPICY TOFU
WITH RICE

Serves: 6

Prep: 15 mins, plus marinating

Cook: 15 mins

Ingredients

250 g/9 oz firm tofu, drained and cut into 1-cm/½-inch cubes

4 tbsp vegetable or groundnut oil

1 tbsp grated fresh ginger

3 garlic cloves, crushed

4 spring onions, thinly sliced

1 head of broccoli, cut into florets

1 carrot, cut into batons

1 yellow pepper, deseeded and thinly sliced

250 g/9 oz shiitake mushrooms, thinly sliced

cooked rice, to serve

Marinade

5 tbsp vegetable stock

2 tsp cornflour

2 tbsp light soy sauce

1 tbsp caster sugar

pinch of chilli flakes

Method

1 Combine all the marinade ingredients in a large bowl. Add the tofu and toss well to cover in the marinade. Set aside to marinate for 20 minutes.

2 Meanwhile, heat a wok or large, heavy-based saucepan over a medium–high heat and add 2 tablespoons of the oil. Fry the tofu with its marinade, stirring constantly, until brown and crispy. Remove from the wok and set aside.

3 Heat the remaining 2 tablespoons of oil in the wok and fry the ginger, garlic and spring onions for 30 seconds. Add the broccoli, carrot, yellow pepper and mushrooms and cook for 5–6 minutes. Return the tofu to the wok and fry to reheat. Serve immediately with the rice.

CHICKPEA & CASHEW NUT CURRY

Serves: 4　　　　**Prep: 15 mins**　　　　**Cook: 40–45 mins**

Ingredients

150 g/5½ oz potatoes

3 tbsp vegetable oil

1 onion, chopped

2 garlic cloves, chopped

3-cm/1¼-inch piece fresh ginger, finely chopped

1 tsp cumin seeds

1 tsp chilli powder

½ tsp turmeric

400 g/14 oz canned chickpeas, drained

150 g/5½ oz cashew nuts

350 ml/12 fl oz vegetable stock

100 g/3½ oz creamed coconut

chopped fresh coriander, to garnish

cooked rice, to serve

Method

1　Dice the potatoes and place in a large saucepan of boiling water. Cook for 10–15 minutes, until tender but still firm.

2　Heat the oil in a large, heavy-based saucepan over a medium heat. Fry the onion, garlic, ginger, cumin seeds, chilli powder and turmeric for 5 minutes, or until the onion is soft.

3　Stir in the boiled potatoes, chickpeas and cashews, and cook for a further 3 minutes. Stir in the stock and the creamed coconut until the coconut melts into the dish. Reduce the heat to low and continue to cook for 15 minutes, or until thick and creamy.

4　Garnish with coriander and serve immediately with cooked rice.

VEGETABLES & PULSES

SPICED ORANGE & CARROT SALAD

Serves: 4

Prep: 25 mins, plus chilling

Cook: No cooking

Ingredients

500 g/1 lb 2 oz carrots, roughly grated

4 spring onions, finely shredded

2 oranges

55 g/2 oz raisins

3 tbsp chopped fresh coriander, plus extra to garnish

Dressing

3 tbsp olive oil

3 tbsp orange juice

2 tsp lemon juice

½ tsp ground cumin

½ tsp ground coriander

salt and pepper

Method

1 Place the carrot and spring onions in a large bowl and toss gently to mix. Using a serrated knife, remove all the peel and pith from the oranges then cut into segments between the membranes. Gently toss the orange segments into the bowl with the raisins and chopped coriander. Stir to mix well.

2 To make the dressing, blend all the ingredients together in a small bowl, or put into a screw-top jar and shake until well blended.

3 Pour the dressing over the carrot salad and toss thoroughly. Cover with clingfilm and chill in the refrigerator for 30 minutes. Adjust the seasoning to taste and serve garnished with coriander.

VEGETABLES & PULSES

SAG ALOO

Serves: 4   **Prep: 15 mins**   **Cook: 40 mins**

Ingredients

500 g/1 lb 2 oz fresh spinach leaves

2 tbsp ghee or vegetable oil

1 tsp black mustard seeds

1 onion, sliced

2 tsp garlic paste

2 tsp ginger paste

900 g/2 lb waxy potatoes, cut into small chunks

1 tsp chilli powder

125 ml/4 fl oz vegetable stock or water

salt

Method

1 Bring a large saucepan of water to the boil. Add the spinach leaves and blanch for 4 minutes. Drain well, then tip into a clean tea towel, roll up and squeeze out the excess liquid.

2 Heat the ghee in a separate saucepan. Add the mustard seeds and cook over a low heat, stirring constantly, for 2 minutes, or until they start to pop. Add the onion, and garlic and ginger pastes and cook, stirring frequently, for 5 minutes, or until softened.

3 Add the potatoes, chilli powder and stock, and season to taste with salt. Bring to the boil, cover and cook for 10 minutes. Add the spinach and stir it in, then cover and simmer for a further 10 minutes, or until the potatoes are tender. Serve immediately.

VEGETABLES & PULSES

SWEET POTATO & LENTIL STEW

Serves: 4 **Prep: 15 mins** **Cook: 30 mins**

Ingredients

2 tbsp vegetable or groundnut oil

350 g/12 oz sweet potato, cut into 1-cm/½-inch cubes

1 onion, chopped

1 carrot, chopped

1 leek, sliced

1 bay leaf

85 g/3 oz Puy lentils

700 ml/1¼ pints vegetable stock

1 tbsp chopped fresh sage

salt and pepper

Method

1 Heat the oil in a large, heavy-based saucepan or stockpot over a low heat. Gently fry the sweet potato, onion, carrot, leek and bay leaf for 5 minutes.

2 Stir in the lentils, stock and sage, and bring to the boil. Reduce the heat and simmer for 20 minutes, or until the lentils are tender but not falling apart.

3 Season to taste with salt and pepper, then remove and discard the bay leaf. Serve immediately.

VEGETABLES & PULSES

SOUTH INDIAN LENTIL BROTH

Serves: 4 **Prep: 10 mins** **Cook: 35–40 mins**

Ingredients

100 g/3½ oz pigeon peas (tuvaar dhal)

600 ml/1 pint cold water

1 tsp ground turmeric

2 tbsp vegetable or groundnut oil

1 tsp black mustard seeds

6–8 fresh curry leaves

1 tsp cumin seeds

1 fresh green chilli

1 tsp tamarind paste

1 tsp salt

cooked rice, to serve

Method

1 Rinse the pigeon peas under cold running water and place in a saucepan with the water, turmeric and 1 tablespoon of the oil. Cover and simmer for 25–30 minutes, or until the peas are cooked and tender.

2 Heat the remaining oil in a frying pan over a medium heat. Add the mustard seeds, curry leaves, cumin seeds, chilli and tamarind paste. When the seeds start to pop, remove the pan from the heat and add to the pea mixture with the salt.

3 Return the broth to the heat for 2–3 minutes. Ladle into small serving bowls and serve immediately with cooked rice.

VEGETABLE NOODLE BROTH

Serves: 4 **Prep: 20 mins** **Cook: 25–30 mins**

Ingredients

400 g/14 oz dried thick egg noodles

2 tbsp vegetable or groundnut oil

1 onion, finely chopped

1 tsp ground cumin

½ tsp ground turmeric

2 garlic cloves, crushed

2 tsp grated fresh ginger

1 tsp salt

2 fresh green chillies, finely chopped

100 g/3½ oz mangetout, thinly sliced lengthways

2 large carrots, cut into matchsticks

1 red pepper, deseeded and thinly sliced

2 tomatoes, finely chopped

2 tbsp dark soy sauce

1 litre/1¾ pints vegetable stock

1 tsp pepper

200 g/7 oz baby spinach leaves

6 tbsp finely chopped fresh coriander

1 tsp toasted sesame oil

Method

1 Cook the noodles according to the packet instructions. Drain, rinse with cold water and set aside.

2 Meanwhile, heat the oil in a large saucepan over a medium heat, add the onion and fry, stirring constantly, for 8–10 minutes, or until lightly browned.

3 Add the cumin, turmeric, garlic, ginger, salt and chillies to the pan, and fry for 1–2 minutes. Add the mangetout, carrots and red pepper and fry for a further 1–2 minutes.

4 Add the tomatoes, soy sauce, stock and pepper Bring to the boil, then reduce the heat and simmer for 10–12 minutes, until the vegetables are tender.

5 Add the reserved noodles and the spinach and bring back to the boil. Stir until the spinach wilts, then remove from the heat and stir in the chopped coriander and sesame oil. Ladle into bowls and serve immediately.

VEGETABLES & PULSES

EGG & LENTIL CURRY

Serves: 4   **Prep: 20 mins**   **Cook: 45 mins**

Ingredients

3 tbsp ghee or vegetable oil

1 large onion, chopped

2 garlic cloves, chopped

2.5-cm/1-inch piece fresh ginger, chopped

½ tsp chilli powder

1 tsp ground coriander

1 tsp ground cumin

1 tsp paprika

85 g/3 oz red split lentils (masoor dhal)

450 ml/16 fl oz vegetable stock

225 g/8 oz canned chopped tomatoes

6 eggs

55 ml/2 fl oz coconut milk

2 tomatoes, cut into wedges

salt

fresh coriander, to garnish

chapatis, to serve

Method

1 Heat a large, heavy-based saucepan over a low heat, then add the ghee. Add the onion and fry for 3 minutes. Stir in the garlic, ginger, chilli and spices and cook, stirring frequently, for 1 minute. Stir in the lentils, stock and tomatoes and bring to the boil. Reduce the heat, cover and simmer, stirring occasionally, for 30 minutes, or until the lentils are tender.

2 Meanwhile, place the eggs in a saucepan of cold water and bring to the boil. Reduce the heat and simmer for 10 minutes. Drain and cover immediately with cold water.

3 Stir the coconut milk into the lentil mixture and season well with salt. Process the mixture in a blender or food processor until smooth. Return to the pan and heat through.

4 Shell the hard-boiled eggs and cut into quarters. Divide the hard-boiled egg quarters and tomato wedges between four serving plates. Spoon over the hot lentil sauce and garnish with the coriander. Serve hot with chapatis.

GARDEN PEAS & PANEER IN CHILLI-TOMATO SAUCE

Serves: 4 **Prep: 20 mins** **Cook: 35–45 mins**

Ingredients

4 tbsp vegetable or groundnut oil

250 g/9 oz paneer, cut into 2.5-cm/1-inch cubes

4 green cardamom pods, bruised

2 bay leaves

1 onion, finely chopped

2 tsp garlic paste

2 tsp ginger paste

2 tsp ground coriander

½ tsp ground turmeric

½–1 tsp chilli powder

150 g/5½ oz canned chopped tomatoes

425 ml/15 fl oz lukewarm water, plus 2 extra tbsp

1 tsp salt, or to taste

125 g/4½ oz frozen peas

½ tsp garam masala

2 tbsp single cream

2 tbsp chopped fresh coriander

naan bread, to serve

Method

1 Heat a medium-sized saucepan over a medium heat, then add 2 tablespoons of the oil. Add the paneer and cook, stirring frequently, for 3–4 minutes, or until evenly browned. Remove from the pan and drain on kitchen paper.

2 Add the remaining oil to the saucepan and reduce the heat to low. Add the cardamom pods and bay leaves, and fry for 20–25 seconds. Add the onion, increase the heat to medium and cook, stirring frequently, for 4–5 minutes until the onion is soft. Add the garlic and ginger pastes and cook, stirring frequently, for a further 3–4 minutes.

3 Add the ground coriander, turmeric and chilli powder and cook, stirring, for 1 minute. Add the tomatoes and cook, stirring frequently, for 4–5 minutes. Add the 2 tablespoons of water and cook, stirring frequently, for 3 minutes, or until the oil separates from the spice paste.

4 Add the remaining water and the salt. Bring to the boil, then reduce the heat to low and simmer, uncovered, for 7–8 minutes. Add the paneer and peas, and simmer for 5 minutes. Stir in the garam masala, cream and chopped coriander, and serve immediately with naan bread.

VEGETABLES & PULSES

RED KIDNEY BEAN CURRY

Serves: 4   **Prep: 20 mins**   **Cook: 25–30 mins**

Ingredients

2 tbsp vegetable or groundnut oil

2 tsp cumin seeds

2 onions, finely chopped

2 tsp grated fresh ginger

6 garlic cloves, crushed

2 fresh green chillies, finely chopped

2 large tomatoes, roughly chopped

2 tsp ground coriander

1 tsp ground cumin

¼ tsp ground turmeric

1 tsp garam masala

800 g/1 lb 12 oz canned red kidney beans, drained and rinsed

1 tsp palm sugar

500 ml/18 fl oz warm water

1 tsp salt

4 tbsp finely chopped fresh coriander, to garnish

natural yogurt, to serve

Method

1 Heat the oil in a large saucepan and add the cumin seeds. When they stop popping, add the onions and fry until soft.

2 Add the ginger and garlic and fry for 2 minutes. Add the green chillies, tomatoes, ground coriander, cumin, turmeric and garam masala and fry, stirring frequently, for 12–15 minutes.

3 Add the red kidney beans, palm sugar, water and salt and cook, for 10–12 minutes, or until the beans are soft.

4 Remove from the heat and transfer to a serving dish. Garnish with the chopped coriander and serve with a dollop of yogurt.

SPICED BENGAL GRAM

Serves: 4 **Prep: 20 mins** **Cook: 40–45 mins**

Ingredients

250 g/9 oz split yellow lentils (chana dhal)

850 ml/1½ pints cold water, plus extra if needed

75 g/2¾ oz ghee

1 small onion, very finely diced

2 fresh green chillies, slit lengthways

1 tbsp ground coriander

1 tsp ground cumin

2 bay leaves

1 tsp hot chilli powder

1 tsp ground turmeric

2 dried red chillies

2 garlic cloves, very finely sliced

2 tsp grated fresh ginger

1 tbsp raisins

2 tsp salt

2 tbsp lightly toasted desiccated coconut, to garnish

Method

1 Place the lentils in a sieve and rinse under cold running water. Drain. Transfer to a saucepan with the water, stir well and bring to the boil, skimming the surface as necessary to remove the foam. Reduce the heat, cover and simmer, stirring frequently and adding more water if needed, for 35–40 minutes, or until the lentils are just tender.

2 Remove the pan from the heat and use a whisk to break down the lentils. Set aside and keep warm.

3 Meanwhile, heat the ghee in a non-stick frying pan over a medium heat. Add the onion and fry, stirring, for 4–5 minutes.

4 Add the fresh green chillies, ground coriander, cumin, bay leaves, chilli powder, turmeric, dried red chillies, garlic and ginger and fry for 1–2 minutes. Add the raisins, stir and cook for 30 seconds.

5 Remove from the heat and pour the spice mixture over the lentils. Stir in the salt, mix well and heat through. Garnish with the toasted coconut and serve immediately.

SPICED BLACK LENTILS

Serves: 4–6

Prep: 20 mins, plus soaking & cooling

Cook: 3¾ hours

Ingredients

250 g/9 oz whole black lentils (urad dhal sabat)

115 g/4 oz dried red kidney beans

4 garlic cloves, cut in half

4 black cardamom pods, lightly crushed

2 bay leaves

1 cinnamon stick

115 g/4 oz butter

¾ tsp garlic paste

¾ tsp ginger paste

2 tbsp tomato purée

½ tsp chilli powder

pinch of sugar

150 ml/5 fl oz double cream

salt, to taste

fresh coriander sprigs, to garnish

Method

1 Put the lentils and kidney beans in separate bowls with plenty of water to cover and leave to soak for at least 5 hours, but preferably overnight.

2 Meanwhile, put the garlic cloves, cardamom pods, bay leaves and cinnamon stick in a piece of muslin and tie together into a bundle.

3 Drain the lentils and kidney beans separately. Put the kidney beans in a large saucepan and cover with twice their volume of water. Bring to the boil, then cook for 10 minutes. Drain well.

4 Return the kidney beans to the pan, add the black lentils and cover with twice their volume of water. Add the spice bag and bring to the boil over a high heat.

5 Reduce the heat to low, partially cover the pan with a lid and simmer, skimming the surface as necessary to remove the foam, for about 3 hours, until the pulses are tender and resemble a thick paste. Check the pan every 15 minutes, adding extra water if it evaporates before the pulses are tender. When the pulses are almost cooked, remove the spice bag and set aside to cool. Once cooked, mash the pulses against the sides of the pan with a wooden spoon.

Melt the butter in a small frying pan. Add the garlic and ginger pastes and stir for 1 minute. Stir in the tomato purée, chilli powder, sugar and salt and continue simmering for 2–3 minutes.

When the spice bag is cool enough to handle, squeeze all the flavouring juices into the pulses. Stir the butter and spice mixture into the pulses, along with all but 2 tablespoons of the cream. Bring to the boil, then reduce the heat and simmer, stirring occasionally, for 10 minutes.

Transfer the dhal to a serving dish, then swirl over the remaining cream and garnish with coriander sprigs.

SPICY CHICKPEAS

Serves: 2–4   **Prep: 20 mins**   **Cook: 15–20 mins**

Ingredients

400 g/14 oz canned chickpeas, drained

2 potatoes, diced

2 tbsp tamarind paste

6 tbsp water

1 tsp chilli powder

2 tsp sugar

1 tsp salt

1 onion, chopped

1 tomato, sliced, to garnish

2 fresh green chillies, chopped, to garnish

2–3 tbsp chopped fresh coriander, to garnish

Method

1. Place the drained chickpeas in a large bowl.

2. Put the potatoes in a saucepan, cover with water and boil until cooked through. Drain and set aside.

3. Mix together the tamarind paste and water in a small bowl.

4. Add the chilli powder, sugar and salt to the tamarind paste mixture and mix together. Pour the mixture over the chickpeas.

5. Add the onion and the diced potatoes, and stir to mix. Season with a little more salt to taste, if necessary.

6. Transfer to a serving bowl and garnish with the sliced tomato, chillies and chopped coriander.

VEGETABLES & PULSES

LENTILS WITH FRESH CHILLIES, MINT & CORIANDER

Serves: 4

Prep: 15 mins,
plus soaking

Cook: 35–40 mins

Ingredients

85 g/3 oz red split lentils

85 g/3 oz split chickpeas

3 tbsp sunflower oil

1 onion, finely chopped

2–3 fresh green chillies, chopped

2 tsp garlic paste

2 tsp ginger paste

1 tsp ground cumin

600 ml/1 pint water

1 tsp salt, or to taste

1 tbsp chopped fresh mint

1 tbsp chopped fresh coriander

55 g/2 oz unsalted butter

1 fresh green chilli and 1 small tomato, cut into julienne strips, to garnish

Method

1 Wash the lentils and chickpeas together until the water runs clear and leave to soak for 30 minutes.

2 Heat a medium-sized saucepan, preferably non-stick, over a medium heat, then add the oil. Add the onion, chillies, and garlic and ginger pastes. Stir-fry the mixture until it begins to brown.

3 Drain the lentils and chickpeas and add to the onion mixture together with the cumin. Reduce the heat to low and stir-fry for 2–3 minutes, then pour in the water. Bring to the boil, reduce the heat to low, cover and simmer for 25–30 minutes.

4 Stir in the salt, mint, coriander and butter. Stir until the butter has melted, then remove from the heat. Serve hot, garnished with chilli and tomato strips.

VEGETABLES & PULSES

MUNG DHAL

Serves: 4

Prep: 15 mins, plus soaking

Cook: 20 mins

Ingredients

225 g/8 oz mung beans or green lentils

3 tbsp vegetable or groundnut oil

1 large onion, chopped

2 garlic cloves, crushed

2.5-cm/1-inch piece fresh ginger, grated

1 tsp ground turmeric

2 small fresh red chillies, deseeded and finely chopped

400 ml/14 fl oz cold water

2 tbsp desiccated coconut

1 tbsp cumin seeds

1 tsp black mustard seeds

salt and pepper

chapatis, to serve

Method

1 Place the mung beans in a bowl and cover with water. Leave to soak for 5 hours or overnight, then drain.

2 Heat the oil in a large, heavy-based saucepan. Add the onion, garlic and ginger, and fry over a medium heat for 5 minutes, to soften.

3 Add the turmeric and chillies and fry for a further minute. Add the soaked mung beans with the cold water and season to taste. Bring to the boil, then reduce the heat and allow to simmer for 10 minutes, or until the water is almost completely absorbed.

4 Meanwhile, place the coconut, cumin and mustard seeds in a frying pan. Dry-fry for about 1 minute until the coconut is golden, then stir into the cooked dhal. Serve hot with chapatis.

LENTILS WITH CUMIN & SHALLOTS

Serves: 4   **Prep: 15 mins**   **Cook: 1 hour**

Ingredients

200 g/7 oz red split lentils (masoor dhal)

850 ml/1½ pints water

1 tsp salt, or to taste

2 tsp vegetable or groundnut oil

½ tsp black mustard seeds

½ tsp cumin seeds

4 shallots, finely chopped

2 fresh green chillies, chopped

1 tsp ground turmeric

1 tsp ground cumin

1 fresh tomato, chopped

2 tbsp chopped fresh coriander

Method

1 Wash the lentils until the water runs clear and put into a medium-sized saucepan. Add the water and bring to the boil. Reduce the heat to medium and skim off any foam. Cook, uncovered, for 10 minutes. Reduce the heat to low, cover and cook for 45 minutes, stirring occasionally to ensure the lentils do not stick to the base of the pan as they thicken. Stir in the salt.

2 Meanwhile, heat a small saucepan over a medium heat and add the oil. When hot, but not smoking, add the mustard and cumin seeds. Add the shallots and chillies and cook, stirring, fo 2–3 minutes, then add the turmeric and ground cumin. Add the tomato and cook, stirring, for 30 seconds.

3 Fold the shallot mixture into the cooked lentils. Stir in the coriander, remove from the heat and serve immediately.

BHEL POORI

Serves: 4

Prep: 20 mins, plus chilling

Cook: 20 mins

Ingredients

300 g/10½ oz new potatoes

200 g/7 oz canned chickpeas, drained

100 g/3½ oz sev noodles

55 g/2 oz puffed rice

4 tbsp raisins

2 tbsp chopped fresh coriander

1 tbsp fennel seeds, toasted and cooled

pooris, crushed

salt

Chaat masala

1 tbsp coriander seeds

1 tbsp cumin seeds

1 tsp black peppercorns

2 dried red chillies

To serve

natural yogurt

tamarind chutney

coriander chutney

Method

1 Bring a large saucepan of salted water to the boil and cook the potatoes for 12–15 minutes, until tender. Drain and run under cold water to cool, then peel and cut into 5-mm/¼-inch dice. Cover and chill for at least 30 minutes.

2 To make the chaat masala, heat a dry frying pan over a high heat. Add the coriander and cumin seeds, peppercorns and chillies and stir until they release their aroma. Immediately tip them out of the pan to stop the cooking. Grind the toasted spice mixture in a spice grinder or mortar.

3 Using a large spoon, carefully toss together the potatoes, chickpeas, sev noodles, puffed rice, raisins, coriander, fennel seeds and crushed pooris. Sprinkle with the chaat masala and toss again.

4 Divide the mixture between small serving bowls and drizzle to taste with the yogurt and chutney. Serve straight away.

CHICKPEAS IN COCONUT MILK

Serves: 4　　　**Prep: 15 mins**　　　**Cook: 15-18 mins**

Ingredients

275 g/9¾ oz potatoes, cut into 1-cm/½-inch cubes

250 ml/9 fl oz hot water

400 g/14 oz canned chickpeas, drained and rinsed

250 ml/9 fl oz coconut milk

1 tsp salt, or to taste

2 tbsp vegetable or groundnut oil

4 large garlic cloves, crushed

2 tsp ground coriander

½ tsp ground turmeric

½–1 tsp chilli powder

juice of ½ lemon

cooked rice, to serve

Method

1　Put the potatoes in a medium saucepan with the hot water. Bring to the boil, then reduce the heat to low and cook, covered, for 6–7 minutes. Add the chickpeas and cook, uncovered, for 3–4 minutes, until the potatoes are tender. Add the coconut milk and salt, and bring to a slow simmer.

2　Meanwhile, place another small saucepan over a low heat and add the oil. Add the garlic and cook, stirring frequently, until it begins to brown. Add the coriander, turmeric and chilli powder and cook, stirring, for 25–30 seconds.

3　Fold the aromatic oil into the chickpeas. Stir in the lemon juice and remove from the heat. Serve hot with rice.

★ **Variation**

To add some extra sweetness to this savoury dish, try using sweet potato instead of white, but only boil for 5–7 minutes in total.

MEAT

PISTACHIO CHICKEN KORMA

Serves: 4

Prep: 20 mins,
plus soaking & marinating

Cook: 50–60 mins

Ingredients

115 g/4 oz shelled
pistachio nuts

200 ml/7 fl oz boiling water

good pinch of saffron
threads, pounded

2 tbsp hot milk

700 g/1 lb 9 oz skinless,
boneless chicken breasts,
cut into large chunks

1 tsp salt, or to taste

½ tsp pepper

juice of ½ lemon

55 g/2 oz ghee or
unsalted butter

6 green cardamom pods

1 large onion,
finely chopped

2 tsp garlic paste

2 tsp ginger paste

1 tbsp ground coriander

½ tsp chilli powder

280 g/10 oz natural yogurt

150 ml/5 fl oz single cream

2 tbsp rosewater

6–8 white rose petals,
washed, to garnish

cooked rice, to serve

lemon wedges, to serve

Method

1 Put the pistachio nuts and boiling water into a heatproof bowl and leave to soak for 20 minutes. Meanwhile, soak the saffron in the hot milk.

2 Put the chicken in a large bowl and add the salt, pepper and lemon juice. Rub the mixture into the chicken, then cover and leave to marinate in the refrigerator for 30 minutes.

3 Heat a medium, heavy-based saucepan over a low heat and add the ghee. Add the cardamom pods and, when they have puffed up, add the onion and increase the heat to medium. Cook, stirring frequently, for 8–9 minutes, until the onion is a pale golden colour.

4 Add the garlic and ginger pastes and cook, stirring frequently, for a further 2–3 minutes. Add the coriander and chilli powder and cook, stirring, for 30 seconds. Add the chicken, increase the heat to medium–high and cook, stirring constantly, for 5–6 minutes until the chicken changes colour.

5 Reduce the heat to low, add the yogurt and the saffron and milk mixture. Bring to a slow simmer, cover and cook for 15 minutes. Stir halfway through to ensure that it isn't sticking to the base of the pan.

MEAT

5 Meanwhile, put the pistachio nuts and their soaking water in a blender or food processor and process until smooth. Add to the chicken mixture, followed by the cream. Cover and simmer, stirring occasionally, for a further 15–20 minutes. Stir in the rosewater and remove from the heat. Garnish with the rose petals and serve immediately with cooked rice and lemon wedges.

★ **Variation**

Rose is a strong flavour and can overpower a dish if too much is used. If you prefer, leave out the rosewater and rose petals and garnish with freshly chopped coriander instead.

CHICKEN TIKKA MASALA

Serves: 4

Prep: 20 mins,
plus marinating

Cook: 50–55 mins

Ingredients

600 g/1 lb 5 oz skinless,
boneless chicken breasts,
cut into large chunks

150 ml/5 fl oz natural yogurt

6 tbsp tikka paste

1 tsp brown sugar

1 tbsp vegetable or
groundnut oil

25 g/1 oz butter

1 large onion, chopped

400 g/14 oz canned
chopped tomatoes

1 tbsp tomato purée

150 ml/5 fl oz water

125 ml/4 fl oz single cream

1–2 tbsp mango chutney

handful of fresh
coriander, chopped

cooked rice or
naan bread, to serve

Method

1. Mix together the chicken, yogurt, 2 tablespoons of the tikka paste and the sugar in a large bowl. Cover and leave to marinate for at least 30 minutes or preferably overnight in the refrigerator.

2. Heat the oil and butter in a large frying pan. Add the onion and fry over a medium–low heat for 15 minutes, or until the onion is golden brown. Preheat the grill to high.

3. Add the remaining tikka paste to the onions. Cook for 2 minutes, stirring constantly, then stir in the chopped tomatoes, tomato purée and water. Simmer gently for 15 minutes.

4. Thread the chicken onto metal or pre-soaked wooden skewers and grill, close to the heat, for 15–20 minutes, turning halfway through, or until cooked through and lightly charred.

5. Stir the cream and chutney into the sauce, adding a little more water if it has become too thick, and heat through for 1–2 minutes. Slide the hot chicken off the skewers using a fork and gently stir into the sauce. Sprinkle with the chopped coriander and serve with rice or naan bread.

MEAT

PEPPERED SOUTH INDIAN CHICKEN CURRY

Serves: 4   **Prep: 20 mins**   **Cook: 25–30 mins**

Ingredients

4 tbsp vegetable or groundnut oil

1 tsp black mustard seeds

pinch of asafoetida

8–10 fresh curry leaves

600 g/1 lb 5 oz skinless, boneless chicken thighs, cut into large chunks

2 tsp ground cumin

1 tsp ground coriander

1 tsp ground turmeric

2 tsp salt

2 tbsp pepper

1 tsp chilli powder

200 ml/7 fl oz coconut cream

200 ml/7 fl oz cold water

1 tsp finely grated fresh ginger

juice of 1 lime

6 tbsp chopped fresh coriander

Method

1 Heat the oil in a large, heavy-based saucepan over a medium heat. Add the mustard seeds and, when they start to pop, add the asafoetida and curry leaves and fry for 30 seconds.

2 Add the chicken and fry, stirring, for 4–5 minutes. Add the cumin, ground coriander, turmeric, salt, pepper and chilli powder, and fry for 1–2 minutes.

3 Add in the coconut cream and water, stir to mix well and cook over a low–medium heat for 15–20 minutes, or until the chicken is cooked through.

4 Stir in the ginger, then remove the pan from the heat and stir in the lime juice. Scatter over the chopped coriander and serve immediately.

MEAT

GOAN SPICED CHICKEN

Serves: 4 **Prep: 20 mins** **Cook: 30–40 mins**

Ingredients

6 black peppercorns

3 cloves

2 tsp fennel seeds

4 dried red chillies

1 tsp cardamom seeds

2 tsp white poppy seeds

2 cinnamon sticks

2 tsp salt

1 tsp ground turmeric

1 tsp ground cumin

1 tsp ground coriander

4 tbsp vegetable or groundnut oil

1 onion, finely chopped

3 garlic cloves, crushed

600 g/1 lb 5 oz skinless, boneless chicken thighs, cut into large chunks

400 ml/14 fl oz coconut milk

300 ml/10 fl oz cold water

1 tsp tamarind paste

Method

1 Place a large frying pan over a medium heat and add the peppercorns, cloves, fennel seeds, dried red chillies, cardamom seeds, white poppy seeds and cinnamon sticks. Dry-fry for 1–2 minutes, then remove from the heat and allow to cool.

2 Place the cooled whole spices into a spice grinder or mortar with the salt, turmeric, cumin and ground coriander. Process until ground to a fine powder.

3 Heat the oil in a large, heavy-based saucepan, add the onion and garlic and cook over a medium heat for 2–3 minutes. Increase the heat to high, add the chicken and fry, stirring constantly, for 5–6 minutes, to seal.

4 Tip in the spice mixture and fry for 1–2 minutes, then add the coconut milk and water. Bring to the boil, then reduce the heat to low and simmer gently for 15–20 minutes. Stir in the tamarind paste and cook for a further 2–3 minutes, or until the chicken is cooked through and tender. Serve immediately.

MEAT

COCONUT & LIME CHICKEN

Serves: 2

Prep: 25 mins,
plus marinating

Cook: 12–15 mins

Ingredients

zest and juice of 1 lime

2 tbsp soy sauce

1 tbsp brown sugar

4 skinless, boneless chicken thighs, sliced

2 tbsp coconut oil, melted and cooled

salt

Mango salsa

1 ripe mango, peeled and flesh diced

1 small red chilli, deseeded and finely diced

juice and zest of ½ lime

small bunch of coriander, chopped

handful toasted coconut flakes

Method

1 In a bowl, mix together the lime, soy sauce and sugar. Add the chicken, stirring to coat, then set aside to marinate for 1 hour. Stir in the coconut oil.

2 For the salsa, combine all of the ingredients in a bowl. Cover and set aside to let the flavours infuse. Preheat the grill to high.

3 Thread the chicken pieces onto metal or pre-soaked wooden skewers and season with salt. Pour any leftover marinade into a small frying pan and boil for a couple of minutes to thicken.

4 Place the skewers onto a wire rack with a tray underneath. Cook under the preheated grill for 10–12 minutes, turning halfway through, and basting occasionally with the marinade, until the chicken is golden and cooked through. Drizzle the skewers with any leftover marinade and serve with the mango salsa.

PARSI-STYLE FRIED CHICKEN

Serves: 4

Prep: 25 mins, plus marinating

Cook: 20–25 mins

Ingredients

1 tsp chilli powder

1 fresh green chilli, chopped

2 tsp salt

1 tsp ground cumin

1 tsp ground coriander

2 tsp grated fresh ginger

3 garlic cloves, crushed

1 tbsp white wine vinegar

1 tsp palm sugar

4 tbsp chopped fresh coriander

600 g/1 lb 5 oz skinless, boneless chicken breasts, cut into large chunks

3 eggs

100 g/3½ oz dried white breadcrumbs

vegetable oil, for deep-frying

Method

1 Place the chilli powder, green chilli, salt, ground cumin and coriander, ginger, garlic, vinegar, palm sugar and chopped coriander in a mixing bowl. Add the chicken and stir to mix well. Cover and leave to marinate in the refrigerator for 6–8 hours, or preferably overnight.

2 Beat the eggs in a shallow bowl. Spread out the breadcrumbs on a large plate. Dip the chicken pieces first in the beaten egg, then roll in the breadcrumbs to coat evenly, before shaking off any excess.

3 Heat enough oil for deep-frying in a large, heavy-based saucepan or deep-fryer to 180–190°C/350–375°F or until a cube of bread browns in 30 seconds. Deep-fry the chicken pieces, in batches, for 5–6 minutes, or until crisp, golden and cooked through. Remove with a slotted spoon and drain on kitchen paper. Serve warm.

MEAT

CHICKEN BREASTS WITH COCONUT MILK

Serves: 4

Prep: 20 mins, plus marinating

Cook: 25–30 mins

Ingredients

1 small onion, chopped

1 fresh green chilli, chopped

2.5-cm/1-inch piece fresh ginger, chopped

2 tsp ground coriander

1 tsp ground cumin

1 tsp fennel seeds

1 tsp ground star anise

4 green cardamom pods

½ tsp ground turmeric

½ tsp black peppercorns

½ tsp ground cloves

600 ml/1 pint coconut milk

4 skinless, boneless chicken breasts

vegetable oil, for brushing

fresh coriander sprigs, to garnish

Method

1 Place the onion, chilli, ginger, ground coriander, cumin, fennel seeds, star anise, cardamom pods, turmeric, peppercorns, cloves and 450 ml/16 fl oz of the coconut milk in a food processor and process to make a paste, adding more coconut milk if necessary.

2 Using a sharp knife, slash the chicken breasts several times and place in a large, shallow dish in a single layer. Pour over half the coconut milk mixture and turn to coat completely. Cover with clingfilm and leave to marinate in the refrigerator for at least 1 hour or up to 8 hours.

3 Heat a ridged grill pan, then brush lightly with vegetable oil. Add the chicken, in batches, and cook for 6–7 minutes on each side, or until cooked through.

4 Meanwhile, pour the remaining coconut milk mixture into a saucepan and bring to the boil, stirring occasionally. To serve, arrange the chicken on a warmed serving dish, spoon over a little of the coconut sauce and garnish with coriander sprigs.

MEAT

TANDOORI CHICKEN

Serves: 4

Prep: 25 mins, plus chilling

Cook: 55–60 mins, plus standing

Ingredients

1 whole chicken, weighing 1.5 kg/3 lb 5 oz, skinned

½ lemon

1 tsp salt

25 g/1 oz ghee, melted

fresh coriander sprigs, to garnish

cooked rice, to serve

lemon wedges, to serve

Tandoori masala paste

1 tbsp garlic paste

1 tbsp ginger paste

1 tbsp ground paprika

1 tsp ground cinnamon

1 tsp ground cumin

½ tsp ground coriander

¼ tsp chilli powder

pinch of ground cloves

200 ml/7 fl oz natural yogurt

Method

1 To make the tandoori masala paste, combine the garlic and ginger pastes and dry spices in a bowl and stir in the yogurt. Set aside.

2 Use a small knife to make thin cuts all over the chicken. Rub the lemon half over the chicken, then rub the salt into the cuts. Put the chicken in a deep bowl, add the paste and use your hands to rub it all over and into the cuts. Cover the bowl with clingfilm and chill in the refrigerator for at least 4 hours, but preferably overnight.

3 When you are ready to cook the chicken, preheat the oven to 200°C/400°F/Gas Mark 6. Put the chicken on a rack in a roasting tin, breast-side up, and drizzle over the melted ghee. Roast in the preheated oven for 45 minutes then increase the temperature to its highest setting.

4 Very carefully pour out any fat from the bottom of the tin. Return the chicken to the tin and put back in the oven to roast for a further 10–15 minutes, until the chicken is tender and the juices run clear when a skewer is inserted into the thickest part of the meat.

5 Leave to stand for 10 minutes, covered, then garnish with coriander sprigs and serve with rice and lemon wedges.

MEAT

CHICKEN IN GREEN CHILLI, MINT & CORIANDER SAUCE

Serves: 4   **Prep: 20 mins**   **Cook: 20–25 mins**

Ingredients

25 g/1 oz fresh coriander, chopped

25 g/1 oz fresh spinach, chopped

2.5-cm/1-inch piece fresh ginger, chopped

3 garlic cloves, chopped

2–3 fresh green chillies, chopped

15 g/½ oz fresh mint

1½ tbsp lemon juice

85 g/3 oz natural yogurt

4 tbsp vegetable or groundnut oil

1 large onion, finely chopped

700 g/1 lb 9 oz skinless, boneless chicken thighs or breasts, cut into large chunks

1 tsp ground turmeric

½ tsp sugar

salt

1 small tomato, deseeded and cut into julienne strips, to garnish

cooked rice, to serve

Method

1 Place the coriander, spinach, ginger, garlic, chillies, mint, lemon juice and ½ teaspoon of salt in a food processor or blender and process to a smooth purée. Add a little water, if necessary, to loosen the mixture. Remove and set aside.

2 Whisk the yogurt until smooth (otherwise it will curdle) and set aside.

3 Heat a large, heavy-based saucepan over a medium–high heat, then add the oil. Add the onion and cook for 5–6 minutes, stirring frequently, until soft.

4 Add the chicken and fry over a medium–high heat, stirring constantly, for 2–3 minutes until the meat changes colour. Add the turmeric, sugar and salt to taste, and fry for a further 2 minutes, then reduce the heat to medium and add half the yogurt. Cook for 1 minute and add the remaining yogurt, then continue cooking over a medium heat until the yogurt resembles a thick batter and the oil is visible.

5 Add the puréed ingredients and cook for 4–5 minutes, stirring constantly. Remove from the heat and garnish with the tomato strips. Serve immediately with rice.

MEAT

LAMB IN CINNAMON & FENUGREEK SAUCE

Serves: 4

Prep: 20 mins,
plus marinating

**Cook: 1 hour-
1 hour 10 mins**

Ingredients

700 g/1 lb 9 oz boneless leg or neck end of lamb, cut into large chunks

4 tbsp red wine vinegar

1 tsp salt, or to taste

4 tbsp vegetable or groundnut oil

1 cinnamon stick, halved

5 green cardamom pods, bruised

5 cloves

1 large onion, finely chopped

2 tsp ginger paste

2 tsp garlic paste

2 tsp ground cumin

1 tsp ground turmeric

½–1 tsp chilli powder

225 g/8 oz canned chopped tomatoes

1½ tbsp dried fenugreek leaves

175 ml/6 fl oz lukewarm water

2 tsp ghee or unsalted butter

½ tsp garam masala

fresh coriander sprigs, to garnish

cooked rice, to serve

Method

1 Put the meat in a bowl and rub in the vinegar and salt. Set aside for 30–40 minutes.

2 Heat a medium-sized, heavy-based saucepan over a low heat and add the oil. Add the cinnamon, cardamom pods and cloves. Fry for 25–30 seconds, then add the onion, increase the heat to medium and cook, stirring regularly, until the onion is soft, but not brown.

3 Add the ginger and garlic pastes and cook for a further 2–3 minutes, then add the cumin, turmeric and chilli powder. Cook for 1–2 minutes and add the tomatoes. Increase the heat slightly and continue to cook until the tomatoes are reduced to a paste-like consistency and the oil separates from the paste. Reduce the heat a little towards the end of the cooking time.

4 Add the meat, fenugreek leaves and water. Bring to the boil, reduce the heat to low, cover and simmer for 45–50 minutes, or until the meat is tender.

5 Heat a small saucepan over a low heat, then add the ghee. Stir in the garam masala. Cook for 30 seconds, then fold this spice mixture into the curry. Remove from the heat, garnish with coriander sprigs and serve immediately with rice.

MEAT

KOLHAPURI MUTTON CURRY

Serves: 4

Prep: 20 mins, plus cooling

Cook: 2 hours–2 hours 5 mins

Ingredients

3 tbsp vegetable or groundnut oil

600 g/1 lb 5 oz boneless mutton shoulder, trimmed and cut into large chunks

1 onion, thinly sliced

3 garlic cloves, crushed

1 tbsp finely grated fresh ginger

1 fresh red chilli, finely chopped

1 tsp ground turmeric

12 fresh curry leaves

400 g/14 oz canned chopped tomatoes

500 ml/18 fl oz lamb or chicken stock

100 ml/3½ fl oz coconut cream

3 tbsp finely chopped fresh coriander, plus extra to garnish

Kolhapuri masala

2 tbsp coriander seeds

1 tbsp cumin seeds

1 tsp ground cardamom seeds

4 cloves

2 cinnamon sticks

2 dried red chillies

¼ tsp freshly grated nutmeg

Method

1 First, make the Kolhapuri masala. Place the coriander, cumin and cardamom seeds, cloves and cinnamon sticks in a frying pan over a low heat. Dry-fry the spices for 1 minute. Remove from the heat and allow to cool, then grind to a fine powder in a spice grinder or mortar with the dried red chilli and nutmeg.

2 Heat 1 tablespoon of the oil in a large, heavy-based saucepan over a medium–high heat. Brown the mutton, in batches, for 3–4 minutes, and set aside. Remove the mutton from the pan with a slotted spoon and set aside.

3 Add the remaining oil to the pan and reduce the heat to medium. Cook the onion, stirring, for 2–3 minutes, until softened. Add the garlic, ginger, fresh red chilli, turmeric and curry leaves, and cook for 1 minute.

4 Add the Kolhapuri masala and stir well to combine, then return the mutton to the pan. Add the chopped tomatoes and stock, and bring to the boil. Reduce the heat to low and simmer, uncovered, for 1½ hours, or until the mutton is tender. Stir in the coconut cream and chopped coriander, then cook for a further 10 minutes. Garnish with extra coriander and serve.

MEAT

KASHMIRI KOFTA CURRY

Serves: 4   **Prep: 20 mins**   **Cook: 30 mins**

Ingredients

500 g/1 lb 2 oz lean minced lamb

1 garlic clove, crushed

2.5-cm/1-inch piece fresh ginger, grated

1 fresh red chilli, deseeded and finely chopped

4 tbsp chopped fresh coriander

2 tbsp vegetable or groundnut oil

1 large onion, finely chopped

2 tbsp garam masala

300 ml/10 fl oz water

4 tbsp mango chutney

150 ml/5 fl oz natural yogurt

salt and pepper

Method

1 Mix together the minced lamb, garlic, ginger, chilli, 2 tablespoons of the coriander and seasoning, to taste, in a bowl until well combined. Form into 20 small balls and set aside.

2 Heat the oil in a frying pan set over a medium heat. Add the meatballs and fry for 10 minutes, turning to brown on all sides. Add the onion and cook for 3 minutes until the onion is starting to soften. Add the garam masala and fry for a further minute.

3 Add the water and mango chutney, and allow to simmer for 10 minutes. Stir in the yogurt and heat through but do not allow to boil as the mixture could curdle.

4 Serve hot, sprinkled with the remaining coriander.

MEAT

MARINATED LAMB BROCHETTES

Serves: 4

Prep: 30 mins,
plus marinating & cooling

Cook: 15 mins

Ingredients

g/1 lb 9 oz boned leg of
mb, cut into large chunks

2 tbsp light malt vinegar

½ tsp salt, or to taste

1 tbsp garlic paste

1 tbsp ginger paste

115 g/4 oz natural yogurt

1 tbsp gram flour

1 tsp ground cumin

1 tsp garam masala

½ tsp ground turmeric

3 tbsp vegetable oil, plus
extra for brushing

½ red pepper, diced

½ green pepper, diced

8 shallots, halved

55 g/2 oz butter, melted

lemon wedges, to serve

Method

1 Put the meat in a large bowl and add the vinegar, salt, and garlic and ginger pastes. Mix together, cover and leave to marinate in the refrigerator for 30 minutes.

2 Put the yogurt and gram flour in a separate bowl and beat together with a fork until smooth. Add the cumin, garam masala, turmeric and oil, and mix thoroughly. Add the yogurt mixture to the marinated meat, then add the peppers and shallots, and stir until well blended. Cover and leave to marinate in the refrigerator for 2–3 hours, or overnight.

3 Preheat the grill to high. Line the grill pan with a piece of foil. Brush the rack and four metal skewers with oil.

4 Thread the marinated lamb, peppers and shallots alternately onto the prepared skewers. Place the skewers on the prepared rack and cook under the preheated grill for 4 minutes. Brush generously with half the melted butter and cook for a further 2 minutes. Turn over and cook for 3–4 minutes. Brush with the remaining butter and cook for a further 2 minutes.

5 Serve straight away with the lemon wedges.

MEAT

CORIANDER LAMB KEBABS

Makes: 6

Prep: 25 mins, plus standing

Cook: 5–7 mins

Ingredients

700 g/1 lb 9 oz lamb mince

1 onion, grated

3 tbsp chopped fresh coriander, plus extra to garnish

3 tbsp gram flour

1½ tbsp ground almonds

3 tbsp lemon juice

2 tbsp natural yogurt

2 tsp ground cumin

2 tsp ground coriander

1½ tsp salt

1½ tsp garam masala

1 tsp ground cinnamon

½ tsp pepper

vegetable oil, for brushing

lemon wedges and fresh tomato salsa, to serve

Method

1 Place all the ingredients, except the oil, in a large bowl and use your hands to mix together until combined and smooth. Cover the bowl and leave to stand at room temperature for about 45 minutes.

2 With wet hands, divide the lamb mixture into 24 equal-sized balls. Thread four balls onto six metal skewers, leaving a little space between the pieces.

3 Preheat the grill to high. Lightly brush the grill rack with oil. Add the skewers and grill, turning frequently, for 5–7 minutes, until the lamb is completely cooked through. Serve immediately with lemon wedges and tomato salsa, and garnish with coriander.

MEAT

KASHMIRI LAMB & FENNEL STEW

Serves: 4　　　　**Prep: 20 mins**　　　　**Cook: 2–2¼ hours**

Ingredients

4 tbsp vegetable oil

2 onions, thinly sliced

600 g/1 lb 5 oz
lamb shoulder

4 garlic cloves, crushed

2 tsp grated fresh ginger

1 tbsp ground coriander

tsp Kashmiri chilli powder

1 tsp salt

300 g/10½ oz potatoes

00 ml/18 fl oz lamb stock

0 ml/7 fl oz single cream

4 tbsp ground almonds

sp crushed fennel seeds

6 tbsp chopped
fresh coriander

2 tbsp finely chopped
fresh mint

Method

1　Heat the oil in a large, heavy-based saucepan and cook the onions over a low heat, stirring frequently, for about 15–20 minutes, until lightly browned. Meanwhile, trim the lamb shoulder of any excess fat and cut into large chunks.

2　Increase the heat to high, add the lamb and stir-fry for 4–5 minutes, until sealed. Reduce the heat to medium and add the garlic, ginger, ground coriander, chilli powder and salt. Stir and cook for 1–2 minutes.

3　Halve the potatoes, then add to the pan with the stock, cover and simmer over a low heat for about 1½ hours, or until the lamb is tender.

4　Uncover the pan, increase the heat slightly and stir in the cream and ground almonds. Cook for a further 8–10 minutes, until thickened and reduced. Take care not to boil or the cream will split.

5　Add the crushed fennel seeds to the pan and cook for a further 3–4 minutes. Remove from the heat and stir in the chopped coriander and mint. Serve immediately.

MEAT

SPICED BEEF CURRY WITH COCONUT & YOGURT

Serves: 4

Prep: 20 mins, plus marinating

Cook: 1 hour 20 mins– 1½ hours

Ingredients

675 g/1 lb 8 oz topside or rump steak

3 tbsp vegetable or groundnut oil

2 bay leaves

1 cinnamon stick, halved

3 cloves

6 green cardamom pods, bruised

½ tsp mustard seeds

½ tsp black peppercorns, cracked

2 onions, halved and finely sliced

300 ml/10 fl oz beef stock

2 tsp curry powder

1 tsp garam masala

200 g/7 oz canned chopped tomatoes

75 g/2¾ oz creamed coconut

5 tbsp natural yogurt

fresh coriander sprigs, to garnish

Marinade

3 garlic cloves, crushed

2.5-cm/1-inch piece fresh ginger, finely chopped

1–3 fresh green chillies, finely chopped

Method

1 Cut the beef into 3-cm/1¼-inch cubes and put into a shallow dish. Use a mortar and pestle to grind the marinade ingredients. Tip over the beef, turning to coat, then leave to marinate for at least 1 hour or overnight.

2 Preheat a large wok over a medium–high heat. Add the oil, then the bay leaves, cinnamon, cloves and cardamom pods, and fry for 15 seconds. Add the mustard seeds and peppercorns, and fry for a further 15 seconds.

3 Stir in the onions, then reduce the heat to medium and gently fry for 10–15 minutes, stirring occasionally, until lightly coloured. Add the beef and the marinade. Stir over a medium–high heat for 2–3 minutes, until brown on the outside. Reduce the heat to low and fry for a further 20 minutes, stirring frequently. Add a little of the stock if the meat becomes very dry.

4 Stir in the curry powder and garam masala. Stir in the tomatoes and fry for a further 5 minutes. Pour in the stock, bring to the boil, then simmer for 15 minutes. Reduce the heat to low. Crumble in the creamed coconut and stir, then mix in the yogurt. Simmer for 15–20 minutes, until the beef is tender. Check the seasoning and serve sprinkled with the coriander sprigs.

MEAT

BEEF RENDANG

Serves: 4

Prep: 25 mins,
plus soaking & cooling

Cook: 2 hours

Ingredients

5–6 dried red chillies

2–3 fresh red chillies, roughly chopped

4–5 shallots or 1 large onion, roughly chopped

4 large garlic cloves, roughly chopped

2.5-cm/1-inch piece fresh ginger, roughly chopped

2 tbsp water

1 tsp coriander seeds

1 tsp cumin seeds

55 g/2 oz desiccated coconut

4 tbsp groundnut oil

700 g/1 lb 9 oz casserole beef, trimmed and cut into large chunks

1 tbsp dark soy sauce

1 lemon grass stalk, finely chopped

3 kaffir lime leaves, shredded, plus extra to garnish

½ tsp salt

200 ml/7 fl oz lukewarm water

1 tbsp tamarind juice

400 ml/14 fl oz coconut milk

toasted flaked coconut, to garnish

cooked rice, to serve

Method

1 Soak the dried chillies in boiling water for 10 minutes, then drain and place in a food processor or blender. Add the fresh chillies, shallots, garlic, ginger and water, and blend until the ingredients are smooth.

2 Heat a small, heavy-based saucepan over a medium heat and add the coriander and cumin seeds. Stir for about a minute until they release their aroma, then remove from the pan and let cool. In the same pan, dry-fry the desiccated coconut, stirring constantly, until it is a light brown colour. Remove from the pan and cool, then mix the coconut with the dry-fried spices and grind them in a spice grinder or mortar.

3 Heat a medium-sized saucepan over a medium heat and add the oil. Add the puréed ingredients and cook, stirring regularly, for 5–6 minutes. Add a little water to prevent the mixture sticking and continue to cook for a further 5–6 minutes, adding more water if necessary.

4 Add the meat and increase the heat to medium–high. Stir until the meat changes colour and add the dry-fried coconut mixture, soy sauce, lemon grass, lime leaves and salt. Stir to mix well and pour in the water. Bring to the boil, reduce the heat to low, then cover and simmer

MEAT

for 45 minutes, stirring occasionally to ensure that the mixture does not stick to the base of the pan.

5 Add the tamarind juice and coconut milk, bring to a gentle simmer, cover and cook for a further 45 minutes, or until the meat is tender. Remove the lid and cook over a medium heat, if necessary, to thicken the sauce. Garnish with the toasted coconut and shredded lime leaves, and serve immediately with rice.

CHILLI-CRUSTED STEAK

Serves: 4–6

Prep: 10 mins,
plus chilling & standing

Cook: 25 mins,
plus resting

Ingredients

2 kg/4 lb 8 oz rump steak

Chilli crust

3 tbsp chipotle chilli paste

1 tsp chilli flakes

3 tbsp light muscovado sugar

3 tbsp sherry vinegar

4 tbsp vegetable or groundnut oil

3 garlic cloves, crushed

2 tsp salt

2 tsp pepper

Method

1 Place all of the chilli crust ingredients in a spice grinder or mortar and crush to a fine paste. Alternatively, process in a food processor or blender.

2 Place the chilli rub in a shallow dish and add the steak, turning a few times to coat. Cover and chill in the refrigerator for a minimum of 4 hours, or overnight.

3 Remove from the refrigerator 2 hours before cooking, to allow the meat to return to room temperature.

4 Preheat a ridged grill pan over a medium–high heat and cook for 10 minutes on each side for medium–rare, or until cooked to your liking. Set the steak aside to rest for 5 minutes before serving, cut into slices.

BEEF BALTI

Serves: 4 **Prep: 15 mins** **Cook: 25 mins**

Ingredients

2 tbsp ghee or vegetable oil

1 onion, thinly sliced

1 garlic clove, finely chopped

2.5-cm/1-inch piece fresh ginger, grated

2 fresh red chillies, deseeded and finely chopped

450 g/1 lb rump steak, cut into thin strips

1 green pepper, thinly sliced

1 yellow pepper, thinly sliced

1 tsp ground cumin

1 tbsp garam masala

4 tomatoes, chopped

2 tbsp lemon juice

1 tbsp water

salt

chopped fresh coriander, to garnish

naan bread, to serve

Method

1 Heat 1 tablespoon of the ghee in a large, heavy based frying pan. Add the onion and cook over a low heat, stirring occasionally, for 8–10 minutes, or until golden. Increase the heat to medium, add the garlic, ginger, chillies and steak, and cook, stirring occasionally, for 5 minutes, or until the steak is browned all over. Remove with a slotted spoon, set aside and keep warm.

2 Add the remaining ghee to the pan. Add the peppers and cook over a medium heat, stirring occasionally, for 4 minutes, or until softened. Stir in the cumin and garam masala and cook, stirring, for 1 minute.

3 Add the tomatoes, lemon juice and water. Season to taste with salt and simmer, stirring constantly, for 3 minutes. Return the steak mixture to the pan and heat through. Transfer to a serving dish, garnish with the coriander and serve immediately with naan bread.

MEAT

MASAMAN CURRY

Serves: 4   **Prep: 15 mins**   **Cook: 15–20 mins**

Ingredients

2 tbsp vegetable or groundnut oil

225 g/8 oz shallots, roughly chopped

1 garlic clove, crushed

450 g/1 lb beef fillet, cut into large chunks

2 tbsp masaman curry paste

3 potatoes, cut into cubes

400 ml/14 fl oz coconut milk

2 tbsp soy sauce

150 ml/5 fl oz beef stock

1 tsp palm sugar

85 g/3 oz unsalted peanuts

2 tbsp chopped fresh coriander, to serve

cooked noodles, to serve

Method

1 Heat a large, heavy-based saucepan over a medium–high heat, then add the oil. Add the shallots and garlic and fry for 1–2 minutes until soft. Add the beef and curry paste and fry over a high heat, for 2–3 minutes, until browned all over. Add the potatoes, coconut milk, soy sauce, stock and sugar, and bring gently to the boil, stirring occasionally. Reduce the heat and simmer for 8–10 minutes until the potatoes are tender.

2 Meanwhile, heat a separate saucepan over a medium–high heat. Add the peanuts and dry-fry, shaking the pan frequently, for 2–3 minutes until lightly browned. Add to the curry with the coriander and stir well. Serve hot with noodles.

BEEF MADRAS

Serves: 4–6　　　**Prep: 20 mins**　　　**Cook: 1 hour 55 mins–2 hours**

Ingredients

1–2 dried red chillies, finely chopped

2 tsp ground coriander

2 tsp ground turmeric

1 tsp black mustard seeds

½ tsp ground ginger

¼ tsp ground pepper

140 g/5 oz creamed coconut, grated and dissolved in 300 ml/ 10 fl oz boiling water

55 g/2 oz ghee or unsalted butter

2 onions, chopped

3 large garlic cloves, chopped

700 g/1 lb 9 oz lean stewing steak, trimmed and cut into large chunks

250 ml/9 fl oz beef stock

lemon juice

salt

fresh coriander sprigs, to garnish

cooked rice, to serve

poppadoms, to serve

Method

1 Put the chopped chillies in a small bowl with the ground coriander, turmeric, mustard seeds, ginger and pepper, and stir in a little of the coconut mixture to make a thin paste.

2 Heat the ghee in a large frying pan with a tight-fitting lid over a medium–high heat. Add the onions and garlic and cook, for 5–8 minutes, stirring frequently, until the onions are golden brown. Add the spice paste and stir for 2 minutes or until it releases its aroma.

3 Add the meat and stock and bring to the boil. Reduce the heat to its lowest setting, cover tightly and simmer for 1½ hours, or until the beef is tender. Check occasionally that the meat isn't catching on the base of the pan and stir in a little extra water or stock, if necessary.

4 Uncover the pan and stir in the remaining coconut milk with the lemon juice and salt, to taste. Bring to the boil, stirring, then reduce the heat again and simmer, still uncovered, until the sauce reduces slightly. Garnish with sprigs of coriander and serve with freshly cooked rice and poppadoms.

KHEEMA MATAR

Serves: 4–6   **Prep: 15 mins**   **Cook: 30–35 mins**

Ingredients

25 g/1 oz ghee or unsalted butter

2 tsp cumin seeds

1 large onion, finely chopped

1 tbsp garlic paste

1 tbsp ginger

2 bay leaves

1 tsp medium curry powder

2 tomatoes, deseeded and chopped

1 tsp ground coriander

¼–½ tsp chilli powder

¼ tsp ground turmeric

pinch of sugar

½ tsp salt

½ tsp pepper

500 g/1 lb 2 oz lean minced beef or lamb

250 g/9 oz frozen peas

Method

1 Heat a large frying pan with a tight-fitting lid over a medium–high heat, then add the ghee. Add the cumin seeds and cook, stirring, for 30 seconds, or until they start to pop.

2 Stir in the onion, garlic and ginger pastes, bay leaves and curry powder, and continue to fry until the fat separates.

3 Stir in the tomatoes and cook for 1–2 minutes. Stir in the coriander, chilli powder, turmeric, sugar, salt and pepper, and stir for 30 seconds.

4 Add the beef, using a wooden spoon to break it up, and cook for 5 minutes, or until the meat is no longer pink. Reduce the heat and simmer, stirring occasionally, for 10 minutes.

5 Add the peas and continue simmering for a further 10–15 minutes, until the peas are thawed and hot. If there is too much liquid left in the pan, increase the heat and leave it to bubble for a few minutes until it reduces. Serve immediately.

PORK VINDALOO

Serves: 4-6

Prep: 20 mins, plus cooling

Cook: 55 mins–1 hour 20 mins

Ingredients

4 tbsp mustard oil

2 large onions, finely chopped

6 bay leaves

6 cloves

6 garlic cloves, chopped

3 green cardamom pods, bruised

1–2 fresh red chillies, chopped

2 tbsp ground cumin

½ tsp salt

½ tsp ground turmeric

2 tbsp cider vinegar

2 tbsp water

1 tbsp tomato purée

700 g/1 lb 9 oz boneless shoulder of pork, trimmed and cut into large chunks

Method

1 Put the mustard oil in a large frying pan or saucepan with a tight-fitting lid over a high heat and heat until it smokes. Turn off the heat and leave the mustard oil to cool completely.

2 Reheat the oil over a medium–high heat. Add the onions and cook, stirring frequently, for 5–8 minutes until softened, but not brown.

3 Add the bay leaves, cloves, garlic, cardamom pods, chillies, cumin, salt, turmeric and 1 tablespoon of the vinegar to the onions, and stir well. Stir in the water, then cover the pan and simmer for about 1 minute, or until the water is absorbed.

4 Dissolve the tomato purée in the remaining vinegar, then stir it into the pan. Add the pork and mix. Add just enough water to cover the pork and bring to the boil. Reduce the heat to its lowest setting, cover the pan tightly and simmer for 40–60 minutes, until the pork is tender.

5 If too much liquid remains in the pan once the pork is cooked, use a slotted spoon to remove the meat and boil the liquid until it reduces to the required amount. Return the pork to the pan to heat through, then transfer to warmed dishes and serve.

MEAT

HONEY & GINGER PORK CHOPS

Serves: 4

Prep: 15 mins,
plus cooling

Cook: 35–40 mins

Ingredients

4 lean pork loin chops

salt and pepper

Honey-ginger glaze

4 tbsp clear honey

1 tbsp dry sherry

4 tbsp orange juice

grated rind of 1 orange

tbsp olive oil, plus extra for brushing and oiling

.5-cm/1-inch piece fresh ginger, grated

Method

1 Preheat the grill to high. Season the pork chops with salt and pepper and set aside.

2 To make the honey–ginger glaze, place the honey, sherry, orange juice, orange rind, olive oil and the ginger in a small saucepan. Bring to the boil, stirring constantly, then reduce the heat and simmer for 15 minutes, or until thickened. Remove from the heat and leave to cool.

3 Oil the grill rack and lightly brush the chops with oil. Cook for 5 minutes on each side, then remove, brush the chops with the glaze and return to the grill to cook for a further 2–4 minutes on each side, basting frequently.

4 Transfer the pork chops to serving plates and serve immediately.

MEAT

PORK WITH TAMARIND

Serves: 6

Prep: 20 mins, plus soaking

Cook: 1¼ hours

Ingredients

55 g/2 oz dried tamarind, chopped

500 ml/18 fl oz boiling water

2 fresh green chillies, deseeded and roughly chopped

2 onions, roughly chopped

2 garlic cloves, roughly chopped

1 lemon grass stalk, bulb end roughly chopped

2 tbsp ghee or unsalted butter

1 tbsp ground coriander

1 tsp ground turmeric

1 tsp ground cardamom

1 tsp chilli powder

1 tsp ginger paste

1 cinnamon stick

1 kg/2 lb 4 oz pork fillet, diced

1 tbsp chopped fresh coriander

fresh coriander sprigs, to garnish

sliced fresh red chillies, to garnish

naan bread, to serve

Method

1 Place the dried tamarind and boiling water in a small bowl and mix well. Leave to soak for 30 minutes.

2 Sieve the soaking liquid into a clean bowl, pressing down the tamarind with the back of a wooden spoon. Discard the pulp. Pour 1 tablespoon of the tamarind liquid into a food processor and add the green chillies, onions, garlic and lemon grass, and process until smooth.

3 Heat the ghee in a large, heavy-based saucepan over a medium heat. Add the ground coriander, turmeric, cardamom, chilli powder, ginger paste, cinnamon stick and the chilli and onion paste, then cook, stirring, for 2 minutes, or until the spices release their aroma.

4 Add the pork and cook, stirring constantly, until lightly browned and well coated in the spice mixture. Pour in the remaining tamarind liquid, bring to the boil, then reduce the heat, cover and simmer for 30 minutes. Remove the lid from the saucepan and simmer for a further 30 minutes, or until the pork is tender. Stir in the chopped coriander. Garnish with sprigs of coriander and sliced red chillies, and serve with naan bread.

MEAT

PAPRIKA PORK

Serves: 4   **Prep: 15 mins**   **Cook: 40 mins**

Ingredients

2 tbsp vegetable or groundnut oil

25 g/1 oz butter

675 g/1 lb 8 oz pork fillet, cut into large chunks

1 onion, chopped

1 tbsp paprika

25 g/1 oz plain flour

300 ml/10 fl oz chicken stock

4 tbsp dry sherry

115 g/4 oz mushrooms, sliced

150 ml/5 fl oz soured cream

salt and pepper

Method

1 Heat the oil and butter in a large, heavy-based saucepan. Add the pork and cook over a medium heat, stirring, for 5 minutes, or until browned. Transfer to a plate with a slotted spoon.

2 Add the chopped onion to the saucepan and cook, stirring occasionally, for 5 minutes, or until softened. Stir in the paprika and flour and cook, stirring constantly, for 2 minutes. Gradually stir in the stock and bring to the boil.

3 Return the pork to the saucepan, add the sherry and sliced mushrooms and season to taste with salt and pepper. Cover and simmer gently for 20 minutes, or until the pork is tender. Stir in the soured cream and serve.

MEAT

PORK CURRY WITH CHILLI, GARLIC & VINEGAR

Serves: 4

Prep: 30 mins, plus marinating

Cook: 1¼ hours– 1 hour 25 mins

Ingredients

2–6 dried red chillies, roughly torn

5 cloves

half a cinnamon stick, broken up

4 cardamom pods

½ tsp black peppercorns

¼ nutmeg, lightly crushed

1 tsp cumin seeds

1½ tsp coriander seeds

½ tsp fenugreek seeds

2 tsp garlic paste

1 tbsp ginger paste

3 tbsp cider vinegar

juice of ½ lime

700 g/1 lb 9 oz boned leg of pork, cut into large chunks

4 tbsp vegetable or groundnut oil, plus 2 extra tsp

2 large onions, finely chopped

250 ml/9 fl oz warm water, plus 4 extra tbsp

1 tsp salt, or to taste

1 tsp soft dark brown sugar

2 large garlic cloves, finely sliced

8–10 curry leaves

cooked rice, to serve

fried okra, to serve

Method

1 Grind the first nine ingredients (all the spices) in a spice grinder or mortar to a fine powder. Transfer the ground spices to a bowl and add the garlic and ginger pastes, vinegar and lime juice. Mix together to form a paste.

2 Put the pork in a large bowl and rub about one-quarter of the spice paste into the meat. Cover and leave to marinate in the refrigerator for 30–40 minutes.

3 Heat the 4 tablespoons of oil in a medium-sized, heavy-based saucepan over a medium heat, add the onions and cook, stirring frequently, for 8–10 minutes, until lightly browned. Add the remaining spice paste and cook, stirring constantly, for 5–6 minutes. Add 2 tablespoons of the warm water and cook until it evaporates. Repeat with the extra 2 tablespoons of water.

4 Add the marinated pork and cook over a medium–high heat for 5–6 minutes, until the meat changes colour. Add the salt, sugar and the remaining warm water. Bring to the boil, then reduce the heat to low, cover and simmer for 50–55 minutes, until the meat is tender.

MEAT

5 Meanwhile, heat the 2 extra teaspoons of oil in a very small saucepan or a steel ladle over a low heat. Add the sliced garlic and cook, stirring frequently, until it begins to brown. Add the curry leaves and leave to sizzle for 15–20 seconds. Stir the garlic mixture into the curry. Remove from the heat and serve immediately with cooked rice and fried okra.

RED PORK CURRY WITH PEPPERS

Serves: 4   **Prep: 20 mins**   **Cook: 15–20 mins**

Ingredients

2 tbsp vegetable or groundnut oil

1 onion, roughly chopped

2 garlic cloves, chopped

450 g/1 lb pork fillet, thickly sliced

1 red pepper, cut into squares

175 g/6 oz mushrooms, quartered

2 tbsp red curry paste

115 g/4 oz creamed coconut, chopped

300 ml/10 fl oz pork or vegetable stock

2 tbsp soy sauce

4 tomatoes, peeled, deseeded and chopped

handful of fresh coriander, chopped, plus extra to garnish

cooked rice noodles, to serve

Method

1 Heat a large, heavy-based saucepan over a medium–high heat, then add the oil. Add the onion and garlic and cook, for 1–2 minutes, until soft, but not brown.

2 Add the pork slices and fry, stirring, for 2–3 minutes, until the meat is brown all over. Add the red pepper, mushrooms and curry paste.

3 Dissolve the creamed coconut in the stock and add to the pan with the soy sauce. Bring to the boil and simmer for 4–5 minutes, or until the liquid has reduced and thickened.

4 Add the tomatoes and coriander and cook for 1–2 minutes. Garnish with extra chopped coriander and serve immediately with rice noodles.

★ Variation

The fragrant flavours of red curry paste and creamed coconut in this recipe would also work well with chicken.

FISH & SEAFOOD

COD CURRY

Serves: 4 **Prep: 25 mins** **Cook: 30 mins,**
plus standing

Ingredients

1 tbsp vegetable or
groundnut oil

1 small onion, chopped

2 garlic cloves, chopped

2.5-cm/1-inch piece fresh
ginger, roughly chopped

2 large ripe tomatoes,
peeled and chopped

150 ml/5 fl oz fish stock

1 tbsp medium curry paste

1 tsp ground coriander

400 g/14 oz canned
chickpeas, drained

750 g/1 lb 10 oz cod fillet,
cut into large chunks

4 tbsp chopped
fresh coriander

4 tbsp natural yogurt

salt and pepper

cooked rice,
to serve

Method

1 Heat the oil in a large, heavy-based saucepan over a low heat. Add the onion, garlic and ginger and cook, for 4–5 minutes, until softened. Remove from the heat. Put the onion mixture into a food processor or blender with the tomatoes and fish stock, and process until smooth.

2 Return to the saucepan with the curry paste, ground coriander and chickpeas. Mix together well, then simmer gently for 15 minutes, until thickened.

3 Add the pieces of fish and return to a simmer. Cook for 5 minutes until the fish is just tender. Remove from the heat and leave to stand for 2–3 minutes.

4 Stir in the coriander and yogurt. Season to taste with salt and pepper and serve with freshly cooked rice.

★ **Variation**

Any meaty, white-fleshed fish, such as hake or monkfish would also work well in this dish.

GOAN FISH CURRY

Serves: 4

Prep: 15 mins, plus marinating

Cook: 25–30 mins

Ingredients

4 skinless salmon fillets, about 200 g/7 oz each

1 tsp salt, or to taste

1 tbsp lemon juice

3 tbsp vegetable or groundnut oil

1 large onion, finely chopped

2 tsp garlic paste

2 tsp ginger paste

½ tsp ground turmeric

1 tsp ground coriander

½ tsp ground cumin

½–1 tsp chilli powder

250 ml/9 fl oz coconut milk

2–3 fresh green chillies, sliced lengthways

2 tbsp cider vinegar or white wine vinegar

2 tbsp chopped fresh coriander

cooked rice, to serve

Method

1 Cut each salmon fillet in half and lay them on a plate in a single layer. Sprinkle with half the salt and all of the lemon juice and rub in gently. Cover and leave to marinate in the refrigerator for 15–20 minutes.

2 Heat a large frying pan over a medium heat, then add the oil. Add the onion and cook, stirring frequently, for 8–9 minutes, until golden.

3 Add the garlic and ginger pastes and cook, stirring, for 1 minute, then add the turmeric, ground coriander, cumin and chilli powder and cook, stirring, for a further minute. Add the coconut milk, chillies and vinegar, then add the remaining salt, stir well and simmer, uncovered, for 6–8 minutes.

4 Add the fish and cook gently for 5–6 minutes. Stir in the fresh coriander and remove from the heat. Serve immediately with rice.

FISH IN SPICY COCONUT BROTH

Serves: 6

Prep: 35 mins, plus infusing

Cook: 30 mins

Ingredients

450 g/1 lb tilapia fillets

700 ml/1¼ pints hot water

1 lemon grass stalk

5-cm/2-inch piece fresh ginger

5–6 shallots or 1 large onion, roughly chopped

2 fresh red chillies, roughly chopped

4 large garlic cloves, roughly chopped

4 tbsp vegetable or groundnut oil

1 tsp ground turmeric

1 tsp shrimp paste

1 tbsp fish sauce

500 g/1 lb 2 oz canned bamboo shoots in water

400 ml/14 fl oz coconut milk

salt

To serve

200 g/7 oz rice noodles, cooked

4 hard-boiled eggs

8 dried red chillies, fried in a little oil until slightly blackened

4 spring onions (white part only), chopped

lime wedges, to serve (optional)

fish cakes or fritters

Method

1 Put the fish in a large, heavy-based saucepan and pour in the hot water. Slice half the lemon grass and half the ginger and add to the fish. Bring to the boil, reduce the heat to low and simmer for 5–6 minutes. Switch off the heat, cove the pan and leave the ginger and lemon grass to infuse in the stock for 15–20 minutes.

2 Meanwhile, roughly chop the remaining lemon grass and ginger, put in a food processor or blender with the shallots, red chillies and garlic, and process until mushy.

3 Heat another large, heavy-based saucepan over a medium heat and add the oil. Add the shallot mixture and turmeric and cook, stirring regularly, for 10–12 minutes, reducing the heat fo the last few minutes of cooking. Sprinkle over a little water, if necessary, to prevent the mixture sticking.

4 Strain the fish stock, reserving the fish, and add enough water to make it up to 700 ml/1¼ pints. Pour into the pan along with the shrimp paste and fish sauce. Leave over a low heat while you prepare the bamboo shoots.

5 Drain the bamboo shoots and chop into bite-sized pieces, then add to the pan with the

coconut milk. Add salt to taste; both the shrimp paste and the fish sauce are salty so make sure to taste before adding salt.

Break up the tilapia fillets into small pieces and add to the pan. Simmer, uncovered, for 5–6 minutes.

To serve, place the noodles in a bowl and top it up with the broth. Serve all the other accompaniments separately so that everyone can help themselves.

BENGALI FISH CURRY

Serves: 4

Prep: 15 mins,
plus cooling

Cook: 30–35 mins

Ingredients

2 tsp coriander seeds

1 tsp cumin seeds

4 tbsp mustard oil

800 g/1 lb 12 oz monkfish fillets, cut into large chunks

2 potatoes, cut into thick batons

1 tsp ground turmeric

2 tsp salt

5 fresh green chillies, slit lengthways

1 tbsp panch phoran spice mix

800 ml/1⅓ pints cold water

cooked rice, to serve

Method

1 Dry-fry the coriander and cumin seeds in a small frying pan for 1–2 minutes. Tip the seeds out of the pan and leave to cool, then finely grind in a spice grinder or mortar. Set aside.

2 Heat 2 tablespoons of the mustard oil in a large, heavy-based saucepan until it is just smoking. Remove from the heat and allow to cool, then heat the oil again over a medium heat. Add the fish and fry for 1 minute on each side. Remove with a slotted spoon and set aside.

3 Heat the remaining oil in the pan, add the potatoes and fry, stirring, for 2–3 minutes. Add the turmeric, salt, chillies, panch phoran and the reserved ground spices and fry, stirring, for 1 minute.

4 Pour in the water and bring to the boil. Reduce the heat and simmer for 12–15 minutes, or until the potatoes are just tender. Add the fish to the saucepan and simmer, for 3–4 minutes, or until the fish is cooked through and the flesh flakes easily. Serve immediately with cooked rice.

FISH & SEAFOOD

SEA BREAM WITH CHILLI & GINGER

Serves: 4 **Prep: 20 mins** **Cook: 12 mins**

Ingredients

500 g/1 lb 2 oz sea bream
or perch fillets

1 garlic clove,
finely chopped

1 small red chilli, deseeded
and finely chopped

2 tbsp fish sauce

3 tbsp lemon juice

100 ml/3½ fl oz fish stock

3 spring onions, trimmed
and finely sliced

1 tbsp finely grated
lemon rind

1 tbsp finely grated
fresh ginger

lemon wedges, to serve

cooked noodles,
to serve

Method

1 Make several deep diagonal cuts in the fish on both sides. Put the fish on a heatproof plate that is slightly smaller than your pan. The plate should have a rim.

2 In a separate bowl, mix together the garlic, chilli, fish sauce, lemon juice and stock. Pour over the fish and scatter over the spring onions, lemon rind and ginger.

3 Fill a large, heavy-based saucepan with about 4 cm/1½ inches boiling water. Bring it back to the boil, then set a rack or trivet inside the pan. Put the plate of fish on top of the rack, then cover with a lid. Reduce the heat a little and steam the fish for about 10 minutes, or until cooked through.

4 Lift out the fish and transfer to individual serving plates. Serve immediately with the lemon wedges and noodes.

CHARGRILLED TUNA WITH CHILLI SALSA

Serves: 4

Prep: 25 mins,
plus marinating & cooling

Cook: 20 mins

Ingredients

4 tuna steaks,
about 175 g/6 oz each

grated rind and juice of
1 lime

2 tbsp vegetable or
groundnut oil, plus extra
for oiling

salt and pepper

fresh coriander sprigs, to
garnish

Chilli salsa

2 orange peppers

1 tbsp olive oil

juice of 1 lime

juice of 1 orange

2–3 fresh red chillies,
deseeded and chopped

pinch of cayenne pepper

Method

1 Place the tuna steaks in a large, shallow dish. Sprinkle the lime rind and juice and the oil over the fish. Season to taste with salt and pepper, cover with clingfilm and leave to marinate in the refrigerator for up to 1 hour.

2 To make the chilli salsa, brush the peppers with the olive oil and cook directly over an open gas flame, turning frequently, for 10 minutes, or until the skin is blackened and charred. If you do not have a gas stove, roast the peppers under the grill on a high heat, for 10–15 minutes, turning frequently, until charred. Remove and leave to cool slightly, then peel off the skins and discard the stem and the seeds. Put the peppers into a food processor or blender with the remaining salsa ingredients and process to a purée. Transfer to a bowl and season to taste with salt and pepper. Preheat a ridged grill pan over a high heat.

3 Oil the grill pan, place the tuna steaks in the pan, then cook, for 4–5 minutes on each side, until golden. Transfer to serving plates, garnish with the coriander sprigs and serve immediately with the salsa.

FISH & SEAFOOD

FISH STICKS WITH CHILLI MAYONNAISE

Serves: 4 **Prep: 20 mins** **Cook: 10 mins**

Ingredients

200 g/7 oz plain flour

3 eggs, beaten

140 g/5 oz matzo meal or breadcrumbs

450 g/1 lb firm white fish fillets, cut into strips

vegetable or groundnut oil, for shallow-frying

salt and pepper

Chilli mayonnaise

2 tbsp sweet chilli sauce

4–5 tbsp mayonnaise

Method

1 Place the flour in a wide, shallow dish. Season to taste with salt and pepper and mix together. Place the beaten egg in another bowl. Place the matzo meal in a third wide, shallow dish.

2 Dip the fish pieces into the seasoned flour, then coat in the egg mixture, shaking off any excess, then roll in the matzo meal.

3 Heat the oil in a large frying pan over a medium heat and cook the fish pieces in batches, until they are golden brown and cooked through.

4 To make the chilli mayonnaise, place the chilli sauce and mayonnaise in a bowl and mix together.

5 Transfer the fish to warmed serving plates and serve immediately with the chilli mayonnaise.

FISH & SEAFOOD

PARSI-STYLE BAKED FISH WRAPPED IN BANANA LEAVES

Serves: 4   **Prep: 25 mins**   **Cook: 15–20 mins**

Ingredients

4 thick cod fillets, about 200 g/7 oz each, skinned

2 tsp ground turmeric

1 large fresh banana leaf

Spice paste

2 tsp ground cumin

2 tsp ground coriander

1½ tsp palm sugar

200 ml/7 fl oz coconut cream

4 fresh red chillies, deseeded and chopped

100 g/3½ oz chopped fresh coriander

4 tbsp chopped fresh mint

5 garlic cloves, chopped

1 tsp finely grated fresh ginger

4 tbsp vegetable or groundnut oil

juice of 2 limes

2 tsp salt

Method

1 Preheat the oven to 200°C/400°F/Gas Mark 6.

2 Place the fish fillets in a single layer on a plate and sprinkle over the turmeric. Rub into the fish and set aside.

3 Place the ingredients for the spice paste in a food processer and process until fairly smooth. Set aside.

4 Cut the banana leaf into four 24-cm/9½-inch squares. Soften the banana leaf squares by dipping them into a pan of very hot water for a few seconds. Once the banana leaf squares have become pliant, wipe them dry with kitcher paper and arrange on a work surface.

5 Apply the spice paste liberally to both sides of each piece of fish. Place a piece of fish on top of each banana leaf square and wrap up like a parcel, securing with bamboo skewers or string.

6 Place the parcels on a baking tray and bake in the preheated oven for 15–20 minutes, until cooked through. Transfer to plates and serve immediately.

FISH & SEAFOOD

KERALAN SPICED FISH IN A PARCEL

Serves: 4

Prep: 45 mins, plus draining

Cook: 15–20 mins

Ingredients

4 whole sea bream or small red snapper, about 400 g/14 oz each

juice of 2 limes

1 tsp sea salt flakes

3 shallots, finely chopped

½ fresh green chilli, deseeded and chopped

4-cm/1½-inch piece fresh ginger, finely chopped

1 tsp black peppercorns, crushed

¼–½ tsp cayenne pepper

1 tsp ground turmeric

oil, for brushing

lime wedges, to garnish

thinly sliced red onion, to garnish

Cucumber & radish salsa

2 cucumbers,

1 tsp salt

juice of 1 lime

1 garlic clove, finely chopped

2 tbsp chopped fresh mint

4 tbsp diced radishes

¼ tsp sugar

pepper

Method

1 To make the cucumber and radish salsa, peel the cucumbers and quarter lengthways. Remove the seeds and slice the flesh crossways into small chunks. Put in a sieve over a bowl and sprinkle with the salt. Leave to drain for 1 hour, then rinse and pat dry. Put in a serving bowl and mix with the lime juice, garlic, mint, radishes, sugar and a little pepper. Cover with clingfilm and set aside.

2 Preheat the oven to 200°C/400°F/Gas Mark 6. Clean and scale the fish, removing the heads. Using a sharp knife, make two diagonal slashes on each side of the fish through the thickest part of the flesh. Put in a shallow dish large enough to accommodate them in a single layer. Combine the lime juice and sea salt and rub all over the fish.

3 Put the shallots, chilli, ginger, peppercorns, cayenne and turmeric into a blender, and blend to a paste. Smear the paste over the fish. Brush four pieces of thick foil with oil. Place a fish on each piece. Wrap in a loose parcel, sealing well.

4 Cook the fish in the oven for 10–15 minutes. Turn and cook for a further 5 minutes. Transfer to serving plates, garnish with the lime wedges and onion rings, and serve immediately with the salsa

GRILLED SALMON WITH MANGO & LIME SALSA

Serves: 4   **Prep: 20 mins**   **Cook: 8–10 mins**

Ingredients

2 tbsp lime juice

1 tbsp clear honey

1 tbsp chopped fresh dill

4 salmon fillets,
about 115 g/4 oz each

salt and pepper

boiled new potatoes
and salad leaves,
to serve (optional)

Mango & lime salsa

1 ripe mango, peeled,
stoned and diced

finely grated rind and juice
of 1 lime

2 tbsp desiccated coconut

1 tbsp chopped fresh dill

Method

1 Preheat a grill to high and lay a piece of foil on a grill rack. Mix together the lime juice, honey and dill in a wide dish. Season to taste with salt and pepper.

2 Place the salmon fillets in the dish and turn to coat evenly in the glaze. Arrange on the prepared grill rack and grill for 4–5 minutes on each side, turning once, or until cooked through

3 Meanwhile, prepare the salsa. Mix the mango in a small bowl with the lime rind and juice. Stir in the coconut and dill.

4 Serve the salmon hot, with the salsa spooned over the top and new potatoes and salad leaves alongside, if desired.

BLACKENED SNAPPER WITH PAPAYA RELISH

Serves: 4

Prep: 20 mins, plus cooling

Cook: 25 mins

Ingredients

4 85-g/3-oz snapper fillets

cooking spray, for oiling

rocket leaves, to serve

Sweetcorn & papaya relish

2 tbsp finely chopped onion

1 tsp sugar

2 tbsp white wine vinegar

2 tbsp fresh or canned sweetcorn kernels

¼ tsp finely chopped habanero chilli

100 ml/3½ fl oz water

¼ tsp yellow mustard seeds

pinch of ground turmeric

1 tsp cornflour, blended with a little cold water

50 g/1¾ oz papaya, cut into small cubes

Seasoning mix

¼ tsp paprika

½ tsp onion powder

¼ tsp dried thyme

¼ tsp dried oregano

¼ tsp cayenne pepper

¼ tsp pepper

½ tsp cornflour

Method

1 To make the relish, place the onion, sugar, vinegar, sweetcorn, chilli, water, mustard seeds and turmeric in a small saucepan over a high heat and bring to the boil. Reduce the heat to medium and simmer for 10 minutes, then add the cornflour mixture, stirring constantly, and cook until it has thickened slightly. Stir in the papaya and leave to cool.

2 To make the seasoning mix, put all the ingredients into a small bowl and mix thoroughly.

3 Sprinkle the seasoning mix over the snapper fillet on both sides and pat into the flesh, then shake off any excess. Lay the fillets on a board.

4 Heat a large frying pan over a high heat until smoking. Lightly spray both sides of the fillets with oil, then cook in the hot pan for 2 minutes. Turn the fillets and cook all the way through. (If the fillets are thick, finish the cooking under a preheated grill). Remove the fish from the pan.

5 Serve the fillets on warmed plates, topped with the relish and served with the rocket leaves.

FISH & SEAFOOD

STUFFED SARDINES

Serves: 4

Prep: 40 mins, plus marinating

Cook: 6–8 mins

Ingredients

1 tbsp finely chopped fresh parsley

4 garlic cloves, finely chopped

12 fresh sardines, cleaned and scaled

3 tbsp lemon juice

olive oil, for brushing and oiling

85 g/3 oz plain flour

1 tsp ground cumin

salt and pepper

toasted bread, to serve

mixed salad, to serve

Method

1 Place the parsley and garlic in a bowl and mix together. Spoon the herb mixture into the fish cavities and pat the remainder all over the outside of the fish. Sprinkle with lemon juice and transfer to a large, shallow dish. Cover and leave to marinate in the refrigerator for 1 hour. Meanwhile, preheat the grill to high.

2 Oil the grill rack. Mix together the flour and ground cumin in a bowl, then season to taste with salt and pepper. Spread out the seasoned flour on a large plate and gently roll the sardines in the flour to coat.

3 Brush the sardines with olive oil and cook the fish under the grill for 3–4 minutes on each side. Transfer to serving plates and serve immediately with the bread and salad.

FISH & SEAFOOD

GRILLED RED SNAPPER
WITH GARLIC

Serves: 4   **Prep: 20 mins**   **Cook: 10 mins**

Ingredients

2 tbsp lemon juice

4 tbsp vegetable or groundnut oil, plus extra for oiling

4 whole red snapper or mullet, scaled and gutted

osp chopped fresh herbs h as oregano, marjoram, lat-leaf parsley or thyme, plus extra to garnish

salt and pepper, to taste

2 garlic cloves, finely chopped

lemon wedges, to serve

mixed salad, to serve

Method

1 Preheat the grill to medium. Oil a grill rack. Put the lemon juice, oil and salt and pepper in a bowl and whisk together. Brush the mixture all over the fish and into the cavities, and sprinkle over the chopped herbs. Place on the prepared grill rack.

2 Cook the fish under the grill for about 10 minutes, basting frequently and turning once, until golden brown.

3 Meanwhile, mix together the chopped garlic and extra herbs. Sprinkle the garlic mixture over the cooked fish and serve hot or cold with the lemon wedges and salad leaves.

FISH & SEAFOOD

SWORDFISH WITH COCONUT GLAZE

Serves: 4

Prep: 25 mins,
plus cooling & marinating

Cook: 20–25 mins

Ingredients

4 swordfish steaks,
2 cm/¾ inch thick,
about 175 g/6 oz each

sea salt flakes

2 tbsp vegetable or
groundnut oil, plus extra
for oiling

chopped fresh coriander,
to garnish

Coconut glaze

425 ml/15 fl oz canned
creamed coconut

125 ml/4 fl oz rum

4 tbsp soy sauce

1 tbsp black peppercorns,
cracked

1 cinnamon stick, broken

Method

1 Put the swordfish steaks in a shallow dish in
a single layer. Rub with sea salt flakes and
vegetable oil.

2 Put the coconut glaze ingredients in a small
saucepan and bring to the boil, stirring. Boil
for 12–15 minutes, until reduced by half.
Strain, pour into a shallow dish and leave until
completely cold.

3 Pour the glaze over the swordfish, turning to coat.
Cover and leave to marinate in the refrigerator
for 30–60 minutes.

4 Preheat the grill to medium–high. Oil a grill rack
using a wad of oil-soaked kitchen paper. Drain
the steaks, reserving the glaze. Brush the steaks
with oil on both sides and arrange on the rack.
Cook the fish under the grill, for 5–6 minutes,
until blackened. Turn and cook the other side for
1 minute, or until the flesh changes colour.

5 Meanwhile, pour the glaze into a small
saucepan. Bring to the boil and boil for 3 minutes.
Pour into a small jug, ready to serve as a sauce.

6 Carefully remove the steaks from the rack.
Arrange in a serving dish, sprinkle with the
coriander and serve with the coconut sauce.

FISH & SEAFOOD

SPICY TUNA FISHCAKES

Serves: 4   **Prep: 20 mins**   **Cook: 8–10 mins**

Ingredients

200 g/7 oz canned
tuna in oil, drained

200 g/7 oz mashed
potatoes

2–3 tbsp curry paste

spring onion, trimmed and
finely chopped

1 egg, beaten

4 tbsp plain flour,
plus extra, for shaping

vegetable or groundnut oil,
for frying

salt and pepper

rocket leaves, to serve

lemon wedges, to serve

Method

1 Place the tuna in a large mixing bowl. Add the mashed potatoes, curry paste, spring onion and egg. Season to taste with salt and pepper and mix together.

2 Divide the mixture into four portions and shape each into a ball. Then, on a floured surface, flatten slightly to make a patty shape of your preferred thickness. Season the 4 tablespoons flour to taste with salt and pepper. Dust each fishcake in the seasoned flour.

3 Heat the oil in a large frying pan, add the fishcakes and fry for 3–4 minutes on each side until crisp and golden.

4 Transfer to warmed serving plates and serve immediately with rocket leaves and lemon wedges.

FISH & SEAFOOD

SPICE-RUBBED SEARED TUNA STEAKS

Serves: 4   **Prep: 15 mins**   **Cook: 10 mins**

Ingredients

675 g/1 lb 8 oz tuna fillet

1½ tsp salt

1 tsp ground coriander

1 tsp paprika

¼ tsp cayenne pepper

1½ tbsp pepper

2 tbsp vegetable or groundnut oil

4 lemon wedges, to garnish

cooked asparagus spears, to serve

Balsamic reduction

6 tbsp aged balsamic vinegar

juice of 1 lemon

1 garlic clove, peeled and halved

Method

1 To make the reduction, put all the ingredients into a small saucepan and place over a medium–low heat. Heat until simmering, then cook until the mixture is reduced by half. Remove from the heat and set aside until needed. It will thicken slightly as it cools.

2 Slice the tuna fillet into four equal-sized rectangular steaks. Mix together the salt, coriander, paprika and cayenne pepper in a small bowl. Lay the tuna steaks on a plate and sprinkle the spice mixture evenly all over them.

3 Coat the steaks with the pepper, gently pressing it in so that it adheres to the surface, being careful not to damage the flesh.

4 Place a large, heavy-based frying pan over a medium–high heat. Add the oil and swirl to coat the pan. When it starts to smoke, add the tuna to the pan and sear the steaks for about 1 minute on each side, or until cooked to your liking.

5 Transfer to a chopping board, cut each steak diagonally into 5–6 slices and fan on a plate. Drizzle a small amount of the reduction alongside each steak fan, garnish with lemon wedges and serve with asparagus spears.

MIXED SEAFOOD CURRY

Serves: 4   **Prep: 20 mins**   **Cook: 10–15 mins**

Ingredients

1 tbsp vegetable or groundnut oil

3 shallots, finely chopped

2.5-cm/1-inch piece fresh galangal, peeled and thinly sliced

2 garlic cloves, finely chopped

400 ml/14 fl oz coconut milk

2 lemon grass stalks, snapped in half

4 tbsp fish sauce

2 tbsp chilli sauce

225 g/8 oz raw tiger prawns, peeled and deveined

225 g/8 oz baby squid, cleaned and thickly sliced

225 g/8 oz salmon fillet, skinned and cut into chunks

175 g/6 oz tuna steak, cut into chunks

225 g/8 oz fresh mussels, scrubbed and debearded

fresh chives, to garnish

cooked rice, to serve

Method

1 Heat the oil in a large, heavy-based saucepan or wok with a tight-fitting lid and stir-fry the shallots, galangal and garlic for 1–2 minutes, until they start to soften. Add the coconut milk, lemon grass, fish sauce and chilli sauce. Bring to the boil, lower the heat and simmer for 1–2 minutes.

2 Add the prawns, squid, salmon and tuna, and simmer for 3–4 minutes, until the prawns have turned pink and the fish is cooked.

3 Discard any mussels with broken shells or any that refuse to close when tapped. Add the remaining mussels to the pan and cover with a lid. Simmer for 1–2 minutes, until they have opened. Discard any mussels that remain closed. Garnish with the chives and serve immediately with freshly cooked rice.

SEAFOOD & MANGO CURRY

Serves: 4　　　　**Prep: 15 mins**　　　　**Cook: 15 mins**

Ingredients

2 tbsp vegetable or groundnut oil

1 red onion, finely chopped

2 garlic cloves, crushed

4 tbsp mild curry paste

400 ml/14 fl oz coconut milk

grated rind of 1 lime

3 tbsp ground almonds

400 g/14 oz frozen mixed seafood, defrosted and drained

1 small ripe mango, peeled, stoned and diced

2 tbsp roughly chopped fresh coriander, to garnish

Method

1 Heat the oil in a large, heavy-based saucepan over a medium heat. Add the onion and garlic and fry for 4 minutes, to soften. Add the curry paste and cook for a further 2 minutes, stirring occasionally.

2 Add the coconut milk and grated lime rind and simmer for 3 minutes. Add the ground almonds and defrosted seafood. Return the pan to the boil then reduce the heat and allow to simmer for 3 minutes, until the seafood is just cooked through.

3 Stir in the diced mango and continue to simmer for 1 minute to heat through. Garnish with the chopped coriander and serve hot.

TANDOORI PRAWNS

Serves: 4

Prep: 25 mins, plus chilling

Cook: 5–6 mins

Ingredients

4 tbsp natural yogurt

2 fresh green chillies, deseeded and chopped

½ tbsp garlic paste

½ tbsp ginger paste

seeds from 4 green cardamom pods

2 tsp ground cumin

1 tsp tomato purée

¼ tsp ground turmeric

¼ tsp salt

pinch of chilli powder

24 raw tiger prawns, thawed if frozen, peeled, deveined and tails left attached

vegetable or groundnut oil, for greasing

Method

1 Put the yogurt, green chillies and garlic and ginger pastes in a small food processor or spice grinder and process to a smooth paste. Transfer the paste to a large bowl and stir in the cardamom seeds, cumin, tomato purée, turmeric, salt and chilli powder.

2 Add the prawns to the bowl and mix well to make sure they are thoroughly coated with the yogurt marinade. Cover the bowl and chill in the refrigerator for at least 30 minutes, or up to 4 hours.

3 When you are ready to cook, heat a large ridged grill pan or frying pan over a high heat. Use crumpled kitchen paper or a pastry brush to very lightly grease the hot pan with oil.

4 Use tongs to lift the prawns out of the marinade, then place the prawns on the grill pan and leave them to cook for 2 minutes. Flip the prawns over and cook for a further 1–2 minutes until they turn pink, curl and are cooked through. Serve immediately.

PRAWN BIRYANI

Serves: 8

Prep: 25 mins, plus soaking

Cook: 25 mins

Ingredients

1 tsp saffron threads

50 ml/2 fl oz tepid water

2 shallots, roughly chopped

3 garlic cloves, crushed

1 tsp chopped fresh ginger

2 tsp coriander seeds

½ tsp black peppercorns

2 cloves

seeds from 2 green cardamom pods

½ cinnamon stick

1 tsp ground turmeric

1 fresh green chilli, chopped

½ tsp salt

2 tbsp ghee or unsalted butter

1 tsp black mustard seeds

500 g/1 lb 2 oz raw tiger prawns, peeled and deveined

300 ml/10 fl oz coconut milk

300 ml/10 fl oz natural yogurt

toasted flaked almonds, to garnish

2 tbsp sliced spring onion, to garnish

fresh coriander sprigs, to garnish

cooked rice, to serve

Method

1 Soak the saffron in the tepid water for 10 minutes. Put the shallots, garlic, ginger, coriander seeds, peppercorns, cloves, cardamom seeds, cinnamon stick, turmeric, chilli and salt into a spice grinder or mortar and grind to a paste.

2 Heat the ghee in a saucepan and add the mustard seeds. When they start to pop, add the prawns and stir over a high heat for 1 minute. Stir in the spice mix, then the coconut milk and yogurt. Simmer for 20 minutes.

3 Spoon the prawn mixture into serving bowls. Top with the freshly cooked rice and drizzle over the saffron water. Serve garnished with the flaked almonds, spring onion and coriander sprigs.

FISH & SEAFOOD

GOAN PRAWN CURRY WITH EGGS

Serves: 4　　　　**Prep: 20 mins**　　　　**Cook: 40–50 mins**

Ingredients

4 tbsp vegetable or groundnut oil

1 large onion, finely chopped

2 tsp ginger paste

2 tsp garlic paste

2 tsp ground coriander

½ tsp ground fennel

½ tsp ground turmeric

½–1 tsp chilli powder

½ tsp pepper

2–3 tbsp water

125 g/4½ oz canned chopped tomatoes

200 ml/7 fl oz coconut milk

1 tsp salt, or to taste

4 hard-boiled eggs

700 g/1 lb 9 oz cooked tiger prawns, peeled

juice of 1 lime

2–3 tbsp chopped fresh coriander

cooked rice, to serve

Method

1　Heat the oil in a medium saucepan over a medium–high heat and add the onion. Cook until the onion is softened, but not browned. Add the ginger and garlic pastes and cook for 2–3 minutes.

2　In a small bowl, mix together the ground coriander and fennel, turmeric, chilli powder and pepper. Add the water and make a paste. Reduce the heat to medium, add this paste to the onion mixture and cook for 1–2 minutes. Reduce the heat to low and continue to cook for 3–4 minutes.

3　Add half the tomatoes and cook for 2–3 minutes. Add the remaining tomatoes and cook for a further 2–3 minutes. Add the coconut milk and salt, bring to a slow simmer and cook, uncovered, for 6–8 minutes.

4　Meanwhile, shell the eggs and, using a sharp knife, make four slits lengthways on each egg without cutting right through. Add the eggs to the pan along with the prawns. Increase the heat slightly and cook for 6–8 minutes.

5　Stir in the lime juice and half the coriander. Transfer the curry to warmed serving dishes. Garnish with the reserved coriander and serve with cooked rice.

FISH & SEAFOOD

PRAWNS WITH GINGER

Serves: 4   **Prep: 15 mins**   **Cook: 25 mins**

Ingredients

1 tsp chopped fresh ginger

1 tsp crushed fresh garlic

1 tsp salt

1 tsp chilli powder

2 tbsp lemon juice

3 tbsp oil

3 onions, chopped

1 green pepper, sliced

400 g/14 oz canned chopped tomatoes

350 g/12 oz cooked, peeled prawns

fresh coriander, to garnish

cooked rice, to serve

Method

1 Place the ginger, garlic, salt and chilli powder in a small bowl and mix to combine. Add the lemon juice and mix to form a paste.

2 Heat the oil in a large, heavy-based saucepan. Add the onions and green pepper, and fry until browned.

3 Add the spice paste to the onions, reduce the heat to low and cook, stirring well, for about 3 minutes. Add the tomatoes and cook for 5–7 minutes, stirring occasionally.

4 Add the prawns to the pan and cook for 10 minutes, stirring occasionally. Garnish with fresh coriander and serve with rice.

PRAWN & RICE SALAD

Serves: 4

Prep: 20 mins,
plus cooling

Cook: 35 mins

Ingredients

175 g/6 oz mixed
long-grain and wild rice

350 g/12 oz cooked,
peeled prawns

1 mango, peeled,
stoned and diced

4 spring onions, sliced

25 g/1 oz flaked almonds

1 tbsp finely chopped
fresh mint

salt and pepper

Dressing

1 tbsp extra virgin olive oil

2 tsp lime juice

1 garlic clove, crushed

1 tsp clear honey

salt and pepper

Method

1 Cook the rice in a large saucepan of lightly salted boiling water for 35 minutes, or until tender. Drain and transfer to a large bowl, then add the prawns and stir to combine.

2 To make the dressing, blend all the ingredients together in a small bowl, or put into a screw-top jar and shake until well blended. Pour the dressing over the rice and prawn mixture, and leave to cool.

3 Add the mango, spring onions, almonds and mint to the salad, and season to taste with pepper. Stir thoroughly, transfer to serving dishes and serve immediately.

PRAWN TIKKA WITH PINEAPPLE

Makes: 4

Prep: 20 mins, plus soaking & marinating

Cook: 8 mins

Ingredients

1 tsp cumin seeds

1 tsp coriander seeds

½ tsp fennel seeds

tsp yellow mustard seeds

¼ tsp fenugreek seeds

¼ tsp nigella seeds

pinch of chilli powder

pinch of salt

2 tbsp lemon or pineapple juice

12 raw tiger prawns, peeled, deveined and tails left attached

12 bite-sized wedges of esh or canned pineapple

chopped fresh coriander, to garnish

Method

1 Heat a large frying pan over a high heat and dry-fry the cumin, coriander, fennel, mustard, fenugreek and nigella seeds, stirring constantly, until the spices release their aroma. Immediately tip the spices out of the pan so they do not burn.

2 Put the spices in a spice grinder or mortar, add the chilli powder and salt, and grind to a fine powder. Transfer to a bowl and stir in the lemon juice.

3 Add the prawns to the bowl and stir so they are well coated, then set aside to marinate for 10 minutes. Meanwhile, preheat the grill to high.

4 Thread three prawns and three pineapple wedges alternately onto each metal or pre-soaked wooden skewer. Cook under the grill for 2 minutes on each side, brushing with any leftover marinade, until the prawns turn pink and are cooked through.

5 Serve the prawns and pineapple tikka garnished with coriander.

FISH & SEAFOOD

PRAWN & SCALLOP KEBABS

Serves: 4

Prep: 25 mins, plus marinating

Cook: 4–6 mins

Ingredients

12 scallops, corals attached, trimmed and cleaned

4–5 tbsp olive oil, plus extra for greasing

juice of 1 lime

24 raw tiger prawns, peeled, deveined and tails left attached

salt and pepper

lime wedges, to garnish

Method

1 Remove the tough muscle from the side of the scallops. Slice in half lengthways through the coral.

2 Combine the oil and lime juice in a shallow dish. Season to taste with salt and pepper. Add the scallops and prawns, and leave to marinate for 15 minutes.

3 Preheat the grill to medium–high. Drain the prawns and scallops, reserving the marinade. Thread the prawns and scallops alternately onto 8 metal or pre-soaked wooden skewers.

4 Cook the kebabs under the grill, turning frequently and brushing with the reserved marinade, for 4–6 minutes, or until cooked through and the prawns have turned pink. Arrange on a serving dish and garnish with lime wedges.

SPICY SCALLOPS WITH LIME & CHILLI

Serves: 4　　　　　**Prep: 20 mins**　　　　　**Cook: 5 mins**

Ingredients

16 large scallops, trimmed and cleaned

1 tbsp butter

1 tbsp vegetable or groundnut oil

1 tsp crushed garlic

1 tsp grated fresh ginger

1 bunch of spring onions, finely sliced

finely grated rind of 1 lime

1 small red chilli, deseeded and finely chopped

3 tbsp lime juice

lime wedges, to serve

cooked rice, to serve

Method

1 Slice each scallop in half horizontally, making two circles from each.

2 Preheat a large, heavy-based saucepan over a medium heat and add the butter and oil.

3 Add the garlic and ginger and fry, stirring constantly, for 1 minute, without browning. Add the spring onions and fry for a further minute.

4 Add the scallops and continue stir-frying over a high heat for 1–2 minutes. Stir in the lime rind, chilli and lime juice, and cook for another minute.

5 Transfer the scallops to warmed serving plates, then spoon over the pan juices and serve immediately with lime wedges and freshly cooked rice.

SAFFRON MUSSEL SOUP

Serves: 4–6

Prep: 25 mins,
plus cooling

Cook: 35–45 mins

Ingredients

2 kg/4 lb 8 oz live mussels

150 ml/5 fl oz dry white wine

1 tbsp butter

2 large shallots,
finely chopped

1 leek, halved lengthways
and thinly sliced

pinch of saffron threads

300 ml/10 fl oz double
cream

1 tbsp cornflour, dissolved in
2 tbsp water

2 tbsp chopped
fresh parsley

salt and pepper

Method

1 Scrub the mussels under cold running water and pull off any beards. Discard any mussels with broken shells and any that refuse to close when tapped.

2 Put the mussels in a large, heavy-based saucepan over a high heat with the wine and a little pepper. Cover tightly and cook for 4–5 minutes, or until the mussels open, shaking the pan occasionally. Discard any mussels that remain closed.

3 When they have cooled slightly, remove the mussels from the shells. Strain the cooking liquid through a muslin-lined sieve. Top up the cooking liquid with water to make 1 litre/1¾ pints.

4 Melt the butter in another heavy-based saucepan. Add the shallots and leek, cover and cook until they begin to soften. Stir in the mussel cooking liquid and the saffron. Bring to the boil, reduce the heat and simmer for 15–20 minutes, or until the vegetables are very tender.

5 Add the cream, stir and bring just to the boil. Stir the dissolved cornflour into the soup and boil gently for 2–3 minutes. Add the mussels and cook for 1–2 minutes. Stir in the parsley and ladle into warmed bowls to serve.

LOBSTER COOKED BEACH-STYLE

Serves: 4   **Prep: 20 mins**   **Cook: 10–15 mins**

Ingredients

2–4 lobsters, halved, or
4 lobster tails, the meat
loosened slightly from
its shell

Chilli butter

115 g/4 oz unsalted butter,
softened

3–4 tbsp chopped fresh
coriander

5 garlic cloves, chopped

2–3 tbsp mild chilli powder

juice of 1 lime

salt and pepper

To serve

salad leaves

lime wedges

fresh salsa of your choice

Method

1 Preheat the grill to high. To make the chilli butter,
put the butter in a bowl and mix in the coriander,
garlic, chilli powder and lime juice. Season with
salt and pepper to taste.

2 Rub the chilli butter into the cut side of the
lobster or lobster tails, working it into all the
cracks and crevices.

3 Wrap loosely in foil and place, cut-side up, on
a grill rack. Cook for 10–15 minutes, or until
just cooked through.

4 Serve with the salad leaves, lime wedges
and salsa.

★ Variation

Try cooking this vibrant dish on the barbecue –
wrap the lobsters loosely in foil and place,
cut-side up, over the hot coals for 5–10 minutes,
or until cooked through.

FISH & SEAFOOD

RICE, BREADS & SWEETS

COCONUT RICE

Serves: 4–6

Prep: 10 mins,
plus soaking & cooling

Cook: 20–22 mins,
plus standing

Ingredients

225 g/8 oz basmati rice

450 ml/16 fl oz water

60 g/2¼ oz creamed
coconut

2 tbsp mustard oil

1½ tsp salt

toasted flaked coconut,
to garnish

Method

1 Rinse the basmati rice until the water runs clear, then leave to soak for 30 minutes in fresh water. Drain and set aside.

2 Bring the water to the boil in a small saucepan, stir in the creamed coconut until it dissolves, then set aside.

3 Heat the mustard oil in a large frying pan or saucepan with a lid over a high heat until it smokes. Turn off the heat and leave the mustard oil to cool completely.

4 Reheat the mustard oil over a medium–high heat. Add the rice and stir well. Add the water with the dissolved coconut and bring to the boil.

5 Reduce the heat to its lowest setting, stir in the salt and cover the pan. Simmer, for 8–10 minutes, until the grains are tender and all the liquid is absorbed. Turn off the heat and fluff up the rice with a fork. Re-cover the pan and leave to stand for 5 minutes. Serve garnished with toasted flaked coconut.

★ Variation

For a nutty garnish, replace the toasted flaked coconut with lightly toasted pistachio nuts tossed in ground cinnamon.

PILAU RICE

Serves: 2–4

Prep: 10 mins,
plus soaking

Cook: 25 mins

Ingredients

200 g/7 oz basmati rice

2 tbsp ghee or
unsalted butter

3 green cardamom pods

2 whole cloves

3 black peppercorns

½ tsp salt

½ tsp saffron threads

400 ml/14 fl oz water

Method

1 Rinse the basmati rice until the water runs clear, then leave to soak for 30 minutes in fresh water. Drain and set aside.

2 Heat a heavy-based saucepan over a medium–high heat, then add the ghee. Add the cardamom pods, cloves and peppercorns and fry for 1 minute. Add the rice and fry for a further 2 minutes.

3 Add the salt, saffron and water to the rice mixture and reduce the heat. Cover the pan and leave to simmer over a low heat for 20 minutes until the grains are tender and all the liquid is absorbed.

4 Transfer the rice to a large, warmed serving dish and serve hot.

AUBERGINE & TOMATO RICE

Serves: 4

Prep: 20 mins, plus soaking

Cook: 20–25 mins, plus standing

Ingredients

275 g/9¾ oz basmati rice

4 tbsp vegetable or groundnut oil

25 g/1 oz ghee

4 shallots, finely chopped

2 garlic cloves, finely chopped

1 cinnamon stick

4 green cardamom pods, bruised

3 cloves

2 tsp cumin seeds

1 aubergine, trimmed and cut into small cubes

4 ripe tomatoes, skinned, deseeded and finely chopped

2 tsp salt

1 tsp pepper

600 ml/1 pint boiling water

6 tbsp finely chopped fresh coriander

Method

1 Wash the rice until the water runs clear, then leave to soak for 20 minutes in fresh water. Drain and set aside.

2 Heat the oil and ghee in a heavy-based saucepan over a medium heat. Fry the shallots, garlic, cinnamon stick, cardamom pods, cloves and cumin seeds for 4–5 minutes, until soft and fragrant.

3 Add the aubergine and fry over a medium heat for 4–5 minutes. Add the tomatoes and the reserved rice and stir to mix well. Add the salt and pepper and pour over the water. Bring to the boil, then cover the pan tightly, reduce the heat to low and cook for 10–12 minutes. Remove from the heat and leave to stand, without lifting the lid, for 10 minutes.

4 When ready to serve, fluff up the grains of rice with a fork. Stir in the chopped coriander and serve immediately.

SPICED BASMATI RICE

Serves: 4

Prep: 10 mins, plus soaking

Cook: 12–15 mins, plus standing

Ingredients

225 g/8 oz basmati rice

2 tbsp vegetable or groundnut oil

5 green cardamom pods, bruised

5 cloves

½ cinnamon stick

1 tsp fennel seeds

½ tsp black mustard seeds

2 bay leaves

450 ml/16 fl oz water

1½ tsp salt, or to taste

pepper

Method

1 Rinse the rice until the water runs clear, then leave to soak for 30 minutes in fresh water. Drain and set aside.

2 Heat a large, heavy-based saucepan with a tight-fitting lid over a medium–high heat, then add the oil. Add the spices and bay leaves and stir for 30 seconds. Stir in the rice so the grains are coated with oil. Stir in the water and salt, and bring to the boil.

3 Reduce the heat to its lowest setting and cover the pan tightly. Simmer, without lifting the lid, for 8–10 minutes, until the grains are tender and all the liquid has been absorbed.

4 Turn off the heat and mix the rice with a fork. Season to taste with pepper. Re-cover the pan and leave to stand for 5 minutes before serving.

MINT & CORIANDER RICE WITH TOASTED PINE NUTS

Serves: 4

Prep: 15 mins, plus soaking

Cook: 15–20 mins, plus standing

Ingredients

good pinch of saffron threads, pounded

2 tbsp hot milk

225 g/8 oz basmati rice

2 tbsp vegetable or groundnut oil

1 cinnamon stick, broken in half

4 green cardamom pods, bruised

2 star anise

2 bay leaves

450 ml/16 fl oz lukewarm water

3 tbsp chopped fresh coriander

2 tbsp chopped fresh mint

1 tsp salt, or to taste

25 g/1 oz pine nuts

Method

1. Put the saffron threads in a small bowl with the milk and set aside.

2. Wash the rice, then leave to soak for 20 minutes in fresh water. Drain and set aside.

3. Heat a medium, heavy-based saucepan over a low heat, then add the oil. Add the cinnamon, cardamom pods, star anise and bay leaves, and leave to sizzle gently for 20–25 seconds. Add the rice and stir well to ensure the grains are coated with the oil.

4. Add the water, stir once and bring to the boil. Add the saffron and milk, coriander, mint and salt and boil for 2–3 minutes. Cover tightly, reduce the heat to very low and cook for 7–8 minutes. Turn off the heat and leave to stand, covered, for 7–8 minutes.

5. Meanwhile, preheat a small heavy-based frying pan over a medium heat, add the pine nuts and cook, stirring, until they are lightly toasted. Transfer to a plate and leave to cool.

6. Add half the pine nuts to the rice and fluff up with a fork. Transfer to a serving dish, garnish with the remaining pine nuts and serve immediately.

LEMON-LACED BASMATI RICE

Serves: 4

Prep: 10 mins,
plus soaking

Cook: 14 mins,
plus standing

Ingredients

225 g/8 oz basmati rice

2 tbsp vegetable or groundnut oil

½ tsp black mustard seeds

10–12 curry leaves, preferably fresh

25 g/1 oz cashew nuts

¼ tsp ground turmeric

1 tsp salt, or to taste

450 ml/16 fl oz hot water

2 tbsp lemon juice

Method

1 Wash the rice until the water runs clear. Leave to soak in fresh cold water for 20 minutes, drain and set aside.

2 Heat a large, heavy-based saucepan over a medium heat, then add the oil. When hot, but not smoking, add the mustard seeds, followed by the curry leaves and the cashew nuts.

3 Stir in the turmeric, quickly followed by the rice and salt. Cook, stirring, for 1 minute, then add the hot water and lemon juice. Stir once, bring to the boil and boil for 2 minutes. Cover tightly, reduce the heat to very low and cook for 8 minutes. Turn off the heat and leave to stand, covered, for 6–7 minutes. Fluff up the rice with a fork and transfer to a serving dish. Serve immediately.

FRUIT & NUT PILAU

Serves: 4–6

Prep: 15 mins,
plus soaking & infusing

Cook: 25–30 mins,
plus standing

Ingredients

225 g/8 oz basmati rice
450 ml/16 fl oz water
½ tsp saffron threads
1 tsp salt
25 g/1 oz ghee
55 g/2 oz almonds
1 onion, thinly sliced
4 green cardamom pods
half a cinnamon stick
1 tsp cumin seeds
1 tsp black peppercorns
2 bay leaves
3 tbsp chopped dried
mango
3 tbsp chopped dried
apricots
2 tbsp sultanas
55 g/2 oz pistachio nuts

Method

1. Wash the rice until the water runs clear, then leave to soak for 30 minutes in fresh water. Drain and set aside.

2. Boil the water in a small saucepan. Add the saffron threads and salt, remove from the heat and set aside to infuse.

3. Heat the ghee in a large, heavy-based saucepan with a tight-fitting lid over a medium–high heat. Add the almonds and stir until golden brown. Remove from the pan using a slotted spoon and set aside.

4. Add the onion to the pan and cook, stirring frequently, for 5–8 minutes until golden, but not brown. Add the seeds from the cardamom pods to the pan with the other spices and bay leaves, and stir.

5. Add the rice and stir until the grains are coated with ghee. Add the saffron-infused water and bring to the boil. Reduce the heat to its lowest setting, stir in the dried fruit and cover the pan tightly. Simmer, without lifting the lid, for 8–10 minutes, until all the liquid is absorbed. Remove from the heat and mix in the almonds and pistachios. Re-cover the pan and leave to stand for 5 minutes before serving.

RICE, BREADS & SWEETS

YELLOW SPLIT MUNG BEAN & RICE PILAF

Serves: 4 **Prep: 10 mins** **Cook: 20–25 mins,**
plus standing

Ingredients

200 g/7 oz split yellow mung beans (moong dhal)

200 g/7 oz basmati rice

25 g/1 oz ghee or unsalted butter

6–8 black peppercorns

2 tsp cumin seeds

4 garlic cloves, finely chopped

2 tsp salt

¼ tsp ground turmeric

1 litre/1¾ pints boiling water

Method

1 Place the mung beans and rice in a sieve and rinse under cold running water. Drain and set aside.

2 Heat the ghee in a large, heavy-based saucepan over a medium heat. Add the mung bean and rice mixture and fry gently for 1–2 minutes.

3 Add the peppercorns, cumin seeds, garlic, salt and turmeric, and fry for 1–2 minutes. Pour in the water.

4 Bring to the boil, then cover tightly and reduce the heat to low. Cook, without stirring, for 12–15 minutes, then remove from the heat (without lifting the lid) and allow to stand for 12–15 minutes.

5 To serve, remove the lid and gently fluff up the grains of rice with a fork. Serve immediately.

KITCHRI

Serves: 4–6

Prep: 15 mins,
plus soaking

Cook: 35–40 mins,
plus standing

Ingredients

225 g/8 oz basmati rice

250 g/9 oz split red lentils
(masoor dhal)

30 g/1 oz ghee or
unsalted butter

1 large onion,
finely chopped

2 tsp garam masala

1½ tsp salt, or to taste

pinch of asafoetida

850 ml/1½ pints cold water

2 tbsp chopped
fresh coriander, plus extra
sprigs to garnish

cucumber raita, to serve

flatbreads, to serve

Method

1 Rinse the rice until the water runs clear, then leave to soak for 30 minutes in fresh water. Drain and set aside.

2 Meanwhile, place the lentils in a sieve and rinse under cold running water. Drain and set aside.

3 Melt the ghee in a flameproof casserole or a large, heavy-based saucepan over a medium–high heat. Add the onion and stir-fry for 5–8 minutes, until golden but not brown.

4 Add the reserved rice and lentils along with the garam masala, salt and asafoetida, and stir for 2 minutes. Pour in the water and bring to the boil, stirring.

5 Reduce the heat to its lowest setting and cover the pan tightly. Simmer, without lifting the lid, for 20 minutes, until the grains are tender and the liquid is absorbed. Re-cover the pan, turn off the heat and leave to stand for 5 minutes.

6 Use a fork to fluff up the grains of rice. Mix in the chopped coriander and adjust the seasoning, adding extra salt if needed. Serve immediately with cucumber raita and flatbreads.

SPICED RICE WITH YOGURT & CUCUMBER

Serves: 4   **Prep: 20 mins**   **Cook: 15 mins, plus standing**

Ingredients

300 g/10½ oz basmati rice

55 g/2 oz ghee or unsalted butter

2 tsp salt

600 ml/1 pint boiling water

2 fresh green chillies, split lengthways and deseeded

1 tbsp finely chopped fresh ginger

4 tbsp cold water

400 ml/14 fl oz natural yogurt, whisked

6 tbsp finely chopped fresh coriander

1 tsp sugar

½ cucumber, finely diced

1 tsp white lentils (urad dhal) (optional)

2 tsp black mustard seeds

2 tsp cumin seeds

2 dried red chillies

6–8 fresh curry leaves

2 garlic cloves, very thinly sliced

Method

1 Place the rice in a large, heavy-based saucepan with 15 g/½ oz of the ghee and 1 teaspoon of the salt and pour over the boiling water. Bring to the boil, then reduce the heat to its lowest setting, cover tightly and simmer for 10–12 minutes. Remove from the heat and allow to stand, without lifting the lid, for 12–15 minutes.

2 Meanwhile, in a spice grinder or mortar, blend together the chillies and ginger with the cold water until smooth.

3 Place the yogurt in a large bowl and add the chilli mixture along with the chopped coriander, sugar, cucumber and the remaining salt. Mix well

4 When the rice has finished standing, uncover and fluff up the grains with a fork. Transfer to a serving dish, spoon over the yogurt mixture and toss to mix well.

5 Melt the remaining ghee in a frying pan. When hot, add the white lentils, if using, and the mustard and cumin seeds. As soon as they start to pop, add the dried red chillies, curry leaves and garlic. Fry for 30–40 seconds, then remove from the heat and pour the spiced oil over the rice mixture. Toss to mix well and serve warm.

RICE, BREADS & SWEETS

CHAPATIS

Makes: 16

Prep: 35 mins, plus resting

Cook: 35 mins

Ingredients

400 g/14 oz chapati flour, plus extra, for dusting

1 tsp salt

½ tsp granulated sugar

2 tbsp vegetable or groundnut oil

250 ml/9 fl oz lukewarm water

Method

1 Mix the flour, salt and sugar together in a large bowl. Add the oil and work well into the flour mixture with your fingertips. Gradually add the water, mixing at the same time. When the dough is formed, transfer to a work surface and knead for 4–5 minutes. The dough is ready when all the excess moisture has been absorbed by the flour. Alternatively, mix the dough in a food processor. Wrap the dough in clingfilm and leave to rest for 30 minutes.

2 Divide the dough in half, then cut each half into eight equal-sized pieces. Form each piece into a ball and flatten into a round cake. Dust each cake lightly in flour and roll out to a 15-cm/6-inch round. Keep the remaining cakes covered while you are working on one. The chapatis will cook better when freshly rolled out, so roll them out and cook them one at a time.

3 Heat a heavy-based cast-iron griddle or a large, heavy-based frying pan over a medium–high heat. Put a chapati on the griddle and cook for 30 seconds. Using a fish slice, turn it over and cook until bubbles begin to appear on the surface. Turn it over again. Press the edges down gently with a clean cloth to encourage the chapati to puff up – they will not always puff up, but this doesn't matter.

RICE, BREADS & SWEETS

Cook until brown patches appear on the underside. Remove from the pan and keep hot by wrapping in a piece of foil lined with kitchen paper. Repeat with the remaining chapatis. Serve warm.

NAAN BREAD

Makes: 10

Prep: 35 mins, plus resting & rising

Cook: 10 mins

Ingredients

900 g/2 lb strong white flour

1 tbsp baking powder

1 tsp sugar

1 tsp salt

300 ml/10 fl oz water, heated to 50°C/122°F

1 egg, beaten

55 g/2 oz ghee, melted, plus extra for rolling out and brushing

Method

1 Sift the flour, baking powder, sugar and salt into a large mixing bowl and make a well in the centre. In another bowl, mix together the water and egg, beating until the egg breaks up. Slowly add the liquid mixture to the the dry ingredients, until a stiff, heavy dough forms. Shape the dough into a ball and return it to the bowl.

2 Cover the bowl with a damp tea towel, tucking the ends under the bowl. Set aside to let the dough rest for 30 minutes. Turn out onto a work surface brushed with a little melted ghee and flatten the dough. Gradually sprinkle the dough with the melted ghee and knead to work it in, little by little, until it is completely incorporated. Shape the dough into 10 equal balls.

3 Resoak the towel in hot water and wring it out again, then place it over the dough balls and leave them to rise for 1 hour. Meanwhile, put three baking sheets in the oven and preheat to 230°C/450°F/Gas Mark 8.

4 Use a lightly greased rolling pin to roll the dough balls into teardrop shapes. Lightly grease the hot baking sheets with ghee. Transfer the naans to the baking sheets and cook, for 5–6 minutes, until they are golden.

SPICED GRAM FLOUR FLATBREADS

Makes: 8

Prep: 20 mins,
plus resting

Cook: 25–35 mins

Ingredients

115 g/4 oz wholemeal flour

115 g/4 oz gram flour,
plus extra for dusting

2 tsp salt

2 tbsp finely chopped
fresh coriander

2 fresh red chillies,
finely chopped

2 tsp cumin seeds

1 tsp coriander seeds,
lightly crushed

1 tsp ground turmeric

75 g/2¾ oz ghee or
unsalted butter, melted, plus
extra for brushing

200 ml/7 fl oz cold water

Method

1 Sift the flours and salt into a large mixing bowl,
adding the bran left in the bottom of the sieve.
Add all the remaining ingredients, except the
water. Mix together and gradually add the water
to form a soft, pliable dough. Knead on a lightly
floured surface for 1–2 minutes, then allow to rest
for 10 minutes.

2 Divide the mixture into eight equal-sized balls,
then roll out each into a 12–15-cm/4½–6-inch
round. Brush the top of each with a little extra
melted ghee.

3 Heat a non-stick, cast-iron griddle or heavy-
based frying pan over a medium heat. When
hot, cook the dough rounds, one at a time, for
1–2 minutes on each side, pressing down with a
spatula. Remove from the griddle, transfer to a
plate and cover to keep warm while you cook
the remaining flatbreads. Serve warm.

RICE, BREADS & SWEETS

PORK-STUFFED FLATBREADS

Makes: 8

Prep: 20 mins, plus standing

Cook: 20–25 mins

Ingredients

1 red onion, thinly sliced

2 tbsp olive oil

450 g/1 lb fresh pork mince

1 white onion, finely chopped

2 garlic cloves, finely chopped

1 tbsp tomato purée

1 tsp ground cumin

¼ tsp dried chilli flakes

150 g/5½ oz feta cheese

2 tbsp chopped fresh coriander

salt and pepper

8 flatbreads, to serve

sliced pickled chillies, to serve

Greek-style yogurt, to serve

Method

1 Put the red onion into a bowl, sprinkle with salt and set aside for 20 minutes, to soften. Rinse well, then squeeze dry and set aside.

2 Heat the oil in a frying pan over a medium heat. Add the pork and white onion and fry, stirring to break up the meat, for 5 minutes, or until the pork is brown. Spoon off any excess fat.

3 Add the garlic, tomato purée, cumin, chilli flakes, and salt and pepper to taste, and stir for 1–3 minutes until the pork is cooked through. Stir in the cheese and chopped coriander.

4 Place the flatbreads, one at a time, in a large frying pan over a medium–high heat and heat until warmed through. Place one eighth of the filling along the centre and top with the red onions, pickled chillies, and a dollop of yogurt.

5 Fold the flatbreads over to encase the filling and serve immediately, while still warm.

RICE, BREADS & SWEETS

POORIS

Makes: 12

Prep: 30 mins,
plus resting

Cook: 20–25 mins

Ingredients

225 g/8 oz wholemeal flour,
sifted, plus extra for dusting

½ tsp salt

30 g/1 oz ghee or
unsalted butter, melted

100–150 ml/3½–5 fl oz cold
water

vegetable or groundnut oil,
for deep-frying

Method

1 Put the flour and salt into a bowl and drizzle the ghee over the surface. Gradually stir in the water until a stiff dough forms. Turn out onto a lightly floured surface and knead for 10 minutes, or until it is smooth and elastic. Shape the dough into a ball and place it in a clean bowl, then cover with a damp tea towel and leave to rest for 20 minutes.

2 Divide the dough into 12 equal-sized pieces and roll each into a ball. Flatten each ball between your palms, then thinly roll it out on a lightly floured surface into a 13-cm/5-inch round. Continue with the rest of the dough.

3 Heat enough oil for deep-frying in a large saucepan or deep-fryer to 180–190°C/350–375°F, or until a cube of bread browns in 30 seconds. Drop a poori into the hot oil and fry for about 10 seconds, or until it puffs up. Flip the poori over and spoon some hot oil over the top.

4 Use the spoon to lift the poori from the oil and let any excess oil drip back into the pan. Drain on kitchen paper and serve immediately. Continue cooking until all the pooris have been fried, making sure the oil returns to the correct temperature before you add the next poori.

RICE, BREADS & SWEETS

CHILLI-CORIANDER NAAN

Makes: 8

Prep: 30 mins, plus resting

Cook: 17 mins

Ingredients

450 g/1 lb plain flour

2 tsp sugar

1 tsp salt

1 tsp baking powder

1 egg

250 ml/9 fl oz milk

2 tbsp vegetable or groundnut oil, plus extra for oiling

2 fresh red chillies, chopped

1 tbsp chopped fresh coriander

2 tbsp butter, melted

Method

1 Sift together the flour, sugar, salt and baking powder into a large bowl. Whisk together the egg and milk and gradually add to the flour mixture, stirring with a wooden spoon, until a dough is formed.

2 Transfer the dough to a work surface, make a depression in the centre of the dough and add the oil. Knead for 3–4 minutes, until the oil is absorbed by the flour. Wrap the dough in clingfilm and leave to rest for 1 hour.

3 Divide the dough into eight equal-sized pieces. Form each piece into a ball and flatten into a thick teardrop shape. Cover the dough shapes with clingfilm and leave to rest for 10–15 minutes.

4 Preheat the grill to high. Line a grill rack with a piece of foil and brush with oil.

5 Mix together the chillies and coriander, then divide into eight equal portions and spread a portion on the surface of each naan. Press gently so that the mixture sticks to the dough.

6 Transfer a naan to the prepared grill pan and cook for 1 minute, or until slightly puffed and brown patches appear on the surface.

As soon as they start to brown, turn over and cook the other side for 45–50 seconds until lightly browned. Remove from the grill and brush with the melted butter. Wrap the cooked naans in a clean tea towel while you cook the remaining naans. Serve warm.

★ **Variation**

These naans will soak up any fragrant flavour – try sprinkling with chopped garlic, ginger and fresh coriander instead.

PARATHAS

Makes: 8

Prep: 40 mins,
plus resting

Cook: 20–25 mins

Ingredients

225 g/8 oz wholemeal flour,
sifted, plus extra for dusting

½ tsp salt

150–200 ml/5–7 fl oz cold
water

140 g/5 oz ghee or unsalted
butter, melted

Method

1 Mix together the flour and salt in a large bowl
   and make a well in the centre. Gradually stir in
   enough of the water to make a stiff dough. Turn
   out onto a lightly floured surface and knead for
   10 minutes, or until smooth. Shape the dough
   into a ball and place in a large, clean bowl, then
   cover with a damp tea towel and leave to rest
   for 20 minutes.

2 Divide the dough into eight equal-sized pieces.
   Lightly flour your hands and roll each into a
   ball. Working with one ball of dough at a time,
   roll it out on a lightly floured surface to form a
   13-cm/5-inch round. Brush the top of the dough
   with about 1½ teaspoons of the melted ghee.
   Fold the round in half to make a half-moon
   shape and brush the top with melted ghee. Fold
   the half-moon shape in half again to make a
   triangle. Press the layers together.

3 Roll out the triangle on a lightly floured surface
   into a larger triangle, then cover with a damp
   tea towel and continue until all the dough is
   shaped and rolled.

4 Meanwhile, heat a large, dry frying pan or
   griddle over a high heat until very hot and a
   splash of water 'dances' when it hits the surface.
   Brush a paratha with more melted ghee and

over and brush the surface with melted ghee. Continue cooking until the bottom is golden brown, then flip the paratha over again and smear with more melted ghee. Use a fish slice to press down on the surface of the paratha so it cooks evenly.

5 Brush with more melted ghee and serve immediately, then repeat with the remaining parathas. Parathas are best served as soon as they come out of the pan, but they can be kept warm wrapped in aluminium foil for about 20 minutes.

PARATHAS STUFFED WITH POTATO & CAULIFLOWER

Makes: 8

Prep: 45 mins, plus cooling & resting

Cook: 35–50 mins

Ingredients

225 g/8 oz wholemeal flour

100 g/3½ oz plain flour, plus extra for dusting

1 tsp freshly ground cardamom seeds

2 tsp salt

250 ml/9 fl oz warm buttermilk

150 g/5½ oz ghee or unsalted butter, melted

Filling

2 tbsp vegetable or groundnut oil

2 tsp cumin seeds

1 tbsp hot curry powder

4 garlic cloves, crushed

2 tsp finely grated fresh ginger

150 g/5½ oz cauliflower florets, finely chopped

2 tsp salt

2 potatoes, boiled and roughly mashed

6 tbsp finely chopped fresh coriander

Method

1 First, make the filling. Heat the oil in a large frying pan over a medium heat. Add the cumin seeds, curry powder, garlic, ginger and cauliflower and fry, stirring, for 8–10 minutes, or until the cauliflower has softened. Add the salt and the mashed potatoes and stir well to mix evenly. Remove from the heat and stir in the chopped coriander. Leave to cool.

2 Sift together the flours, ground cardamom seeds and salt into a large bowl, adding the bran left in the bottom of the sieve. Make a well in the centre and pour in the buttermilk and 2 tablespoons of the melted ghee. Work into the flour mixture to make a soft dough. Knead on a lightly floured surface for 10 minutes and form into a ball. Put the dough into a large bowl, cover with a damp cloth and leave to rest for 20 minutes. Divide the dough into eight equal-sized balls, then roll out each into a 15-cm/6-inch round.

3 Place a little of the filling into the centre of each dough round and fold up the edges into the centre to enclose the filling. Press down lightly and, using a lightly floured rolling pin, roll out to make a 15-cm/6-inch paratha. Repeat with the remaining dough and filling.

4 Heat a flat cast-iron griddle or heavy-based frying pan over a medium heat. Brush each paratha with a little of the remaining melted ghee. Brush the griddle with a little melted ghee. Put a paratha in the griddle and cook for 1–2 minutes, pressing down with a spatula. Turn over, brush with a little more ghee and cook for a further for 1–2 minutes. Remove from the griddle, transfer to a plate and cover with foil to keep warm while you cook the remaining parathas. Serve warm.

DOSAS

Makes: 8

Prep: 20 mins,
plus soaking & fermenting

Cook: 45 mins

Ingredients

115 g/4 oz basmati rice, rinsed

70 g/2½ oz split black lentils (urad dhal chilke)

¼ tsp fenugreek seeds

125 ml/4 fl oz water

25 g/1 oz ghee or unsalted butter, melted

salt

Method

1 Bring a saucepan of lightly salted water to the boil, add the rice and boil for 5 minutes, then drain. Put the rice, lentils and fenugreek seeds in a bowl with water to cover, and leave to soak overnight.

2 The next day, strain the rice and lentils, reserving the soaking liquid. Put the rice and lentils in a food processor with 75 ml/2½ fl oz of the water and process until a smooth, sludgy grey paste forms. Slowly add the remaining water.

3 Cover the bowl with a tea towel that has been soaked in hot water and wrung out, and leave to ferment in a warm place for 5–6 hours, until small bubbles appear all over the surface.

4 Stir the mixture and add as much extra water as necessary to achieve the consistency of single cream. Season with salt, to taste. The amount of salt you need depends on how sour-tasting the batter is.

5 Heat a large frying pan over a high heat until a splash of water 'dances' when it hits the surface, then brush the surface with melted ghee. Put a ladleful of batter in the centre of the pan, then leave it to cook for 2 minutes until it is golden brown and crisp.

6 Flip the dosa over and continue cooking for a further 2 minutes. Turn it out of the pan and keep warm. Continue until all the batter has been used. Serve wrapped around a filling or on their own as an accompaniment.

BAKED PASSION FRUIT CUSTARDS

Serves: 4   **Prep: 15 mins**   **Cook: 40–45 mins**

Ingredients

4 passion fruit
4 large eggs
175 ml/6 fl oz coconut milk
55 g/2 oz caster sugar
1 tsp orange flower water

Method

1 Preheat the oven to 180°C/350°F/Gas Mark 4. Halve three passion fruits, scoop out the flesh and rub through a sieve to remove the seeds.

2 In another bowl, beat together the eggs, passion fruit juice, coconut milk, sugar and orange flower water until a smooth custard forms.

3 Pour the custard into four 200-ml/7-fl oz ovenproof dishes. Place in a baking tin and pour in hot water to reach halfway up the dishes.

4 Bake in the oven for 40–45 minutes or until just set Scoop the pulp from the remaining passion fruit and spoon a little onto each dish to serve. Serve the custards slightly warm, or chilled.

CREAMY ALMOND, PISTACHIO & RICE PUDDING

Serves: 4 **Prep: 10 mins** **Cook: 30–35 mins,
plus standing**

Ingredients

2 litres/3½ pints milk

85 g/3 oz basmati rice

100 g/3½ oz golden
caster sugar

1 tsp freshly ground
cardamom seeds

6 tbsp finely chopped
pistachio nuts

6 tbsp finely chopped
blanched almonds

Method

1 Pour the milk into a large, heavy-based
saucepan and bring to the boil.

2 Add the rice and cook over a medium heat,
stirring constantly, for 18–20 minutes, or until the
rice is tender.

3 Add the sugar, stir and cook for a further
3–4 minutes.

4 Remove from the heat and stir in the ground
cardamom and the nuts. Cover and leave to
stand for 20 minutes before serving.

BAKED SPICED PUDDING

Serves: 4–6 **Prep: 20 mins** **Cook: 1 hour 55 mins–2 hours 10 mins**

Ingredients

2 tbsp raisins or sultanas

5 tbsp polenta

350 ml/12 fl oz milk

4 tbsp blackstrap molasses

2 tbsp soft dark brown sugar

½ tbsp salt

30 g/1 oz butter, diced, plus extra, for greasing

2 tsp ground ginger

¼ tsp cinnamon

¼ tsp ground nutmeg

2 eggs, beaten

vanilla ice cream, to serve

Method

1 Preheat the oven to 150°C/300°F/Gas Mark 2. Generously grease a 900-ml/1½-pint ovenproof dish and set aside. Put the raisins in a sieve with 1 tablespoon of the polenta and toss well together. Set aside.

2 Put the milk and molasses into a large, heavy-based saucepan over a medium–high heat and stir until the molasses has dissolved. Add the sugar and salt, and continue stirring until the sugar is dissolved. Sprinkle over the remaining polenta and bring to the boil, stirring constantly. Reduce the heat and simmer for 3–5 minutes, until the mixture is thickened.

3 Remove the pan from the heat, add the butter, ginger, cinnamon and nutmeg, and stir until the butter is melted. Add the eggs and beat until they are incorporated, then stir in the raisins. Pour the mixture into the prepared dish.

4 Put the dish in a small roasting tin and pour in enough boiling water to come halfway up the side of the dish. Put the dish in the preheated oven and bake, uncovered, for 1¾–2 hours, until the pudding is set and a wooden skewer inserted in the centre comes out clean. Serve immediately, with a dollop of ice cream on top.

GOAN LAYERED COCONUT CAKE

Serves: 8–10

Prep: 30 mins, plus cooling & chilling

Cook: 1 hour 50 mins– 2¼ hours

Ingredients

400 ml/14 fl oz coconut milk

300 g/10½ oz golden caster sugar

10 egg yolks, lightly beaten

200 g/7 oz plain flour

½ tsp freshly grated nutmeg

1 tsp freshly ground cardamom seeds

pinch of ground cloves

¼ tsp ground cinnamon

100 g/3½ oz butter, plus extra, for greasing

Method

1 Preheat the oven to 200°C/400°F/Gas Mark 6. Lightly grease a 17-cm/6½-inch round cake tin and line with baking paper.

2 Pour the coconut milk into a saucepan and stir in the sugar. Heat gently for 8–10 minutes, stirring until the sugar has dissolved. Remove from the heat and gradually add the beaten egg yolks, whisking constantly. Sift in the flour and spices and stir to make a smooth batter.

3 Melt the butter, then add a tablespoon to the prepared tin and spread over the base. Pour an eighth of the batter into the tin and spread to coat the base evenly. Bake in the preheated oven for 10–12 minutes, or until set.

4 Remove from the oven and brush another spoonful of the melted butter over the top, followed by another eighth of the batter. Return to the oven and cook for 10–12 minutes, or until set.

5 Repeat until all the butter and batter has been used up, baking for a further 20–25 minutes, or until the top is golden brown and the cake is firmly set. Remove from the oven and allow to cool in the tin. When cool, remove the cake from the tin, cover with clingfilm and chill for 4–6 hours before serving.

RICE, BREADS & SWEETS

ROSE & VERMICELLI MILKSHAKE

Serves: 4

Prep: 15 mins,
plus soaking

Cook: 5 mins

Ingredients

2 tsp edible basil seeds
(tukmaria)

200 ml/7 fl oz cold water

10 g/¼ oz very fine rice
vermicelli (sevai)

125 ml/4 fl oz rose syrup

1 litre/1¾ pints chilled milk

4 scoops of vanilla
ice cream, to serve

Method

1 Place the basil seeds in a bowl and pour over
the water. Leave to soak for 15 minutes, or until
swollen and jelly-like. Drain and set aside.

2 Meanwhile, break the vermicelli into small pieces
and cook according to the packet instructions.
Drain and refresh under cold running water.

3 To assemble the drinks, pour the rose syrup into
the bases of four glasses. Divide the soaked
basil seeds and the drained vermicelli between
the glasses.

4 Pour over the chilled milk and top each with a
scoop of ice cream. Serve immediately.

RICE, BREADS & SWEETS

BENGALI CARAMEL YOGURT

Serves: 4

Prep: 10 mins,
plus chilling

Cook: 15 mins,
plus standing

Ingredients

400 g/14 oz
evaporated milk

200 g/7 oz condensed milk

2 tbsp caster sugar

100 g/3½ oz natural yogurt,
whisked

Method

1 Pour the evaporated milk and condensed milk into a large, heavy-based saucepan set over a medium heat and bring to the boil. Reduce the heat to low, stir and simmer gently for 10 minutes, or until well combined. Remove from the heat.

2 In a separate small saucepan, heat the sugar over a low heat until it starts to melt, turns golden and begins to caramelize. Remove from the heat.

3 Add the caramelized sugar to the milk mixture and stir to mix well. When the milk mixture is just warm, stir in the yogurt and mix well.

4 Pour the mixture into four small serving bowls, cover with clingfilm and leave to stand in a warm place for 8–10 hours or overnight, until lightly set. Transfer to the refrigerator and chill for 4–6 hours before serving.

SALT LASSI

Serves: 4–6   **Prep: 10 mins**   **Cook: No cooking**

Ingredients

700 ml/1¼ pints natural yogurt
½ tsp salt
¼ tsp sugar
250 ml/9 fl oz cold water
ice cubes
ground cumin, to garnish
fresh mint, to garnish
spiced nuts, to serve

Method

1 Beat together the yogurt, salt and sugar in a jug or bowl, then add the water and whisk until frothy.

2 Fill four or six glasses with ice cubes and pour over the yogurt mixture. Lightly dust the top of each glass with ground cumin and decorate with mint. Serve with spiced nuts.

SWEET LASSI

Serves: 4

Prep: 10 mins, plus chilling

Cook: No cooking

Ingredients

500 ml/18 fl oz natural yogurt

225 ml/8 fl oz iced water

4 tbsp caster sugar

crushed ice

finely chopped pistachio nuts, to decorate

Method

1 Pour the yogurt into a bowl and whisk with a balloon whisk or hand-held electric mixer for 1–2 minutes, or until frothy.

2 Add the water and sugar, and whisk until the sugar has dissolved. Pour into a jug, cover with clingfilm and leave to chill in the refrigerator for 30 minutes.

3 Fill four tall glasses with crushed ice and pour in the lassi. Sprinkle with chopped pistachios to decorate and serve immediately.

★ Variation

To make this refreshing drink even more delicious, sprinkle over some sweet cinnamon or nutmeg, or even a few drops of rosewater, to boost the flavour.

INDEX

INDEX

This edition published by Parragon Books Ltd in 2015
LOVE FOOD is an imprint of Parragon Books Ltd

Parragon Books Ltd
Chartist House
15–17 Trim Street
Bath BA1 1HA, UK
www.parragon.com/lovefood

ISBN 978-1-4723-5999-5
Printed in China

Cover photography by Ian Garlick
Introduction by Anne Sheasby

Notes for the Reader
This book uses both metric and imperial measurements. Follow the
same units of measurement throughout; do not mix metric and imperial.
All spoon measurements are level: teaspoons are assumed to be 5 ml,
and tablespoons are assumed to be 15 ml. Unless otherwise stated, milk
is assumed to be full fat, eggs and individual vegetables are medium,
and pepper is freshly ground black pepper. Unless otherwise stated, all
root vegetables should be peeled prior to using.

Garnishes, decorations and serving suggestions are all optional and
not necessarily included in the recipe ingredients or method. The
times given are an approximate guide only. Preparation times differ
according to the techniques used by different people and the cooking
times may also vary from those given. Optional ingredients, variations or
serving suggestions have not been included in the time calculations.

Vegetarians should be aware that some of the ready-made ingredients
used in the recipes in this book may contain animal products. Always
check the packaging before use.